WHAT PEOPLE ARE SAYI
ABOUT OUR BOOKS...

D0204716

*"Trusting a recipe often comes down to trusting the source.
The sources for the recipes are impeccable;
in fact, they're some of the best chefs in the nation."*

BON APPETIT MAGAZINE

"Should be in the library—and kitchen—of every serious cook."

JIM WOOD—Food & Wine Editor—San Francisco Examiner

*"A well-organized and user-friendly tribute
to many of the state's finest restaurant chefs."*

San Francisco Chronicle

*"An attractive guide to the best restaurants and inns, offering recipes
from their delectable repertoire of menus."*

GAIL RUDDER KENT—Country Inns Magazine

"Outstanding cookbook."

HERITAGE NEWSPAPERS

"Nothing caters to visitors as well as this book does."

TONY TOLLNER—Co-owner, Rio Grill

"It's an answer to what to eat, where to eat—and how to do it yourself."

MONTEREY HERALD

*"I dare you to browse through these recipes without being tempted
to rush to the kitchen."*

PAT GRIFFITH—Chief Washington Bureau, Blade Communications Inc.

Books of the "Secrets" Series

MONTEREY'S

Whispered recipes and guide to restaurants, inns and wineries of the Monterey Peninsula.

COOKING SECRETS

by Kathleen DeVanna Fish
with Fred Hernandez

Bon Vivant Press
Monterey, California

Library of Congress Cataloging-in-Publication Data

MONTEREY'S COOKING SECRETS
Whispered Recipes and guide to restaurants, inns and wineries of the Monterey Peninsula

Sixth revised printing 1997

Fish, Kathleen DeVanna
92-074452
ISBN 9620472-6-0
First printing 1993
$13.95 softcover
Includes indexes
Autobiography page

Copyright ©1997 by Kathleen DeVanna Fish

Editorial direction by Fred Hernandez
Cover photography by Robert N. Fish
Cover design by Morris Design
Pat Hathaway Collection of California Views, pages 19, 155, 251
Photos from The Herald, Monterey, pages 75, 159, 225, 241

Published by Bon Vivant Press
a division of The Millennium Publishing Group
P.O. Box 1994
Monterey, CA 93942

Printed in the United States of America

CONTENTS

History, Legend and Lore
North to South

The chefs at the Hotel Del Monte: A proud tradition

CUISINE INDEX

ASIAN

Fishery, 44

AUSTRIAN

Gernot's Victoria House, 118

CALIFORNIA CUISINE

Central 159 Catering, 96
Old Bath House, 128
Pacific's Edge, 192
Portola Cafe, 52
Rio Grill, 206
Sierra Mar, 242
Silver Jones, 218
Tarpy's Roadhouse, 64
Ventana, 246

FRENCH

Club XIX, 164
The Covey, 226
Creme Carmel, 188
Fresh Cream, 48
Melac's, 122
The Ridge Restaurant, 236
Sans Souci, 214

ITALIAN

Bay Club, 160
Cafe Fina, 24
Domenico's, 30
Ferrante's, 40
Pasta Mia, 134
Piatti, 198
Raffaello, 202
Sardine Factory, 56
Vito's, 150
Whaling Station Inn, 68

JAPANESE

Robata Grill & Sake Bar, 206

MEDITERRANEAN

Casanova, 182
Epsilon, 34
Fandango, 106
Taste, 144

MEXICAN

Peppers, 138

SEAFOOD

The Fishwife, 110

SOUTH AMERICAN

El Cocodrilo, 102

GEOGRAPHIC INDEX

FALLING IN LOVE with the Monterey Peninsula is easy to do, especially if you know the secret hideaways.

That's what this book is all about: secrets.

Included are recommendations for unforgettable places to stay—inns with walled gardens and sunset views from Victorian parlors, inns where the visitor enters another world.

Then there is the incomparable food of the Monterey Peninsula. The bulk of this book is about exquisite food. Selections include treasured recipes from the inns and wineries. The restaurants go one step further: they provide full menus and their closely-guarded recipes.

SAVOR SUCH DELICACIES as crab saffron bisque, warm escargot salad, salmon mousse Wellington, P'ad Thai prawns, medallions of veal with pistachio butter sauce, vegetable terrine with cognac or chocolate decadence. Or how about some goat cheese fritters with apricot sauce or roasted garlic you spread like butter.

To make life easy, the book is divided into six geographical zones, from north to south: Monterey, Pacific Grove, Pebble Beach, Carmel, Carmel Valley and Big Sur. Recommended inns and restaurants—and their recipes—are listed for each zone.

Wineries you should know about are listed in a separate section. The wineries offer exceptional ways to cook with wine.

AND, TO HELP YOU get into the spirit of romance and adventure, each zone is introduced with tidbits of history, legend and lore. You'll learn about a lovely walled garden where grizzly bears and bulls fought to the death, about a submarine attack, smugglers, and movie stars dressed up for polo matches.

You'll discover where to enjoy a picnic while watching whales swim by, about sea lions that balance on rocks and look like modern sculptures, butterflies that cover tree branches, the town where blue laws outlawed liquor until 1969, and the real location of Treasure Island.

Discover the magical experience that lies hidden on the Monterey Peninsula. You'll never look at it the same way again.

FAVORITE RESTAURANT RECIPES

BAY CLUB

Menu for Four   160

SALMON AL PIATTO
SAFFRON RISOTTO
LOBSTER WITH ASPARAGUS
IN RED WINE SAUCE

CAFE FINA

Menu for Four   24

OYSTERS ROCKEFELLER
LENTIL SOUP
CABBAGE SALAD WITH PROSCIUTTO
FINA PASTA
RASPBERRY GRANITA

CASANOVA

Menu for Four   182

PESTO SOUP
SMOKED SALMON SALAD
BEEF TENDERLOIN SPAGHETTI
SPINACH WITH CHEESE
CANNOLI ALLA SICILIANA

CENTRAL 159 CATERING

Menu for Six   96

GRILLED ZESTY PRAWNS
SMOKED TROUT CHOWDER
WILTED SPINACH SALAD
TAIPEI GRILLED CHICKEN BREASTS
FLOURLESS CHOCOLATE PECAN CAKE

CLUB XIX

Menu for Four   164

POACHED PEAR AND ENDIVE
SALAD WITH ROQUEFORT CHEESE
AND HAZELNUTS
ABALONE IN TARRAGON
BUTTER SAUCE
CRÈME BRULÉE

COVEY

Menu for Eight 226

LEEK & ONION SOUP

ROULADE OF SOLE AND SALMON

CHICKEN STUFFED
WITH DATES & HAM

CHOCOLATE GRAND MARNIER
MOUSSE TORTE

CREME CARMEL

Menu for Six 188

LOBSTER SOUP

LAMB LOIN WITH ROSEMARY
& GARLIC

APPLE MINT CHUTNEY

CHOCOLATE SOUFFLÉ

DOMENICO'S

Menu for Four 30

TOMATO GINGER SOUP

MARINATED SCALLOPS

SEAFOOD PASTA

EL COCODRILO

Menu for Four 102

SWEET CORN TAMALES

SEAFOOD CALDO

CHICKEN BREAST CRIOLLO

EPSILON

Menu for Four 34

COUNTRY GREEK SALAD

CHICKEN SOUP
WITH EGG LEMON SAUCE

SPANAKOPITA

ALMOND BAKLAVA

FANDANGO

Menu for Six   106

SALADE NIÇOISE
PAELLA
CRÈME BRULÉE

FERRANTE'S

Menu for Four   40

CREAM OF ZUCCHINI SOUP
STUFFED MUSHROOMS
FETTUCCINE FERRANTE'S

THE FISHERY

Menu for Four   44

CURRIED SQUID COCKTAIL
CRISPY FISH IN SWEET & SOUR SAUCE
NUTCRACKER FLAMBÉ

THE FISHWIFE

Menu for Four   110

NEW ZEALAND MUSSELS IN CILANTRO
& SERRANO CREAM
SALSA FRESCA
BOSTON CLAM CHOWDER
MIXED GREENS
WITH ROASTED PECANS
HONEY MUSTARD VINAIGRETTE
TILAPIA CANCUN
CARIBBEAN COLE SLAW
KEY LIME PIE

FRESH CREAM

Menu for Six   48

LOBSTER RAVIOLI
MIXED GREENS
WITH BALSAMIC VINAIGRETTE
CHOCOLATE BAG
WITH ICE CREAM SHAKE

GERNOT'S VICTORIA HOUSE

Menu for Four   118

BATTERED MUSHROOMS
AUSTRIAN WIENER SCHNITZEL
MERINGUE SOUFFLÉ

MELAC'S

Menu for Eight   122

VEGETABLE TERRINE
WITH CURRIED VINAIGRETTE
SEAFOOD CASSOULET
TRUFFLE CAKE

OLD BATH HOUSE

Menu for Six   128

SMOKED PHEASANT
& DUCK CARPACCIO
FRUIT OF THE SEA SALAD
MANGO VINAIGRETTE
VEAL MONARCH
AMARETTO TIRAMISU

PACIFIC'S EDGE

Menu for Four   192

SARDINE FILETS ON POTATOES
WITH ROSEMARY VINAIGRETTE
BEEF TENDERLOIN WITH
CHANTERELLES AND BRAISED LEEKS
ROASTED RACK OF LAMB
TOMATO STUFFED
WITH POTATO RISOTTO
LEMON VERBENA JASMINE ICE CREAM

PASTA MIA

Menu for Four   134

RADICCHIO WALNUT SALAD
CHICKEN PUTTANESCA
WITH POLENTA
ZABAGLIONE FREDDO

PEPPERS

Menu for Four 138

STEAMED CLAMS & MUSSELS
SCALLOP SALAD
CILANTRO VINAIGRETTE
PRAWNS WITH BLACK BEANS
SPANISH RICE, SALSA CRUDA
AVOCADO SALSA

PIATTI RISTORANTE

Menu for Four 198

GORGONZOLA SALAD
FETTUCCINE
WITH CHICKEN AND MUSHROOMS
TIRAMISU WITH CRÈME ANGLAISE

PORTOLA CAFE

Menu for Four 52

CRAB AND SEAFOOD CAKES
ROASTED GARLIC AND CORN FLAN
FRESH BERRY TARTS WITH PASTRY CREAM

RAFFAELLO

Menu for Four 202

FETTUCCINE IN PARMESAN CHEESE
VEAL IN TOMATO WINE SAUCE
CHOCOLATE SOUFFLÉ

THE RIDGE RESTAURANT

Menu for Six 236

THREE ONION SOUP
WITH GRUYÈRE CRUST

SCALLOPS IN FRESH BASIL
& ROMA TOMATO
OVER FETTUCCINE

RACK OF LAMB

RIO GRILL

Menu for Four 206

ROASTED GARLIC
CORN SALAD
GRILLED RABBIT

ROBATA

Menu for Four   210

FILET MIGNON ROLL
SHIITAKE SALMON
VEGGIES WITH SESAME CREAM
BBQ RICE BALL

SANS SOUCI

Menu for Four   214

GOAT CHEESE FRITTERS
APRICOT SAUCE
SALMON WITH GRAPEFRUIT BUTTER
CHOCOLATE CAKE

SARDINE FACTORY

Menu for Four   56

CALAMARI FRITTERS
ESCARGOT EN TOSCANI
PRAWNS BALTINO
PRAWNS SAMBUCCA
SWORDFISH STEAK
WITH SUNDRIED TOMATO
TAPENADE
OSSO BUCO
APPLE FILLED PURSE
WITH CRÈME ANGLAISE

SIERRA MAR

Menu for Four   242

POTATOES STUFFED
WITH SMOKED TROUT MOUSSE

FETTUCCINE WITH OLIVE,
TOMATO & BASIL

VENISON WITH CURRANTS
AND WHITE RAISINS

SILVER JONES

Menu for Six   218

PICO DE GALLO
SWEET PEPPER & TOMATO SOUP
WILD RICE & MUSHROOM SALAD
PENNE PASTA WITH PANCETTA
BREAD PUDDING
WITH JACK DANIELS SAUCE

TARPY'S ROADHOUSE

Menu for Four 64

CAJUN SPICED PRAWNS
ROSEMARY LAMB LOIN
BERRY ANGEL FOOD CAKE

TASTE CAFE & BISTRO

Menu for Six 144

ITALIAN QUESADILLAS
TUSCAN WHITE BEAN SOUP
CHICKEN BREASTS, ARTICHOKES,
FETTUCCINE
STRAWBERRIES
WITH VANILLA GELATO

VENTANA

Menu for Four 246

OAK-SMOKED SALMON
WITH LEMON CRÈME FRAÎCHE
SEARED RABBIT WITH PENNE PASTA
LOBSTER AND MASCARPONE
RAVIOLI WITH TOMATO VINAIGRETTE
& CHANTERELLES

VITO'S

Menu for Four 150

EGGPLANT PARMIGIANA
CANELLONI
ICE CREAM TORTE

WHALING STATION INN

Menu for Four 68

THE FABULOUS ARTICHOKE
SPICY PRAWNS
PASTA WITH PANCETTA & PEAS
GRILLED SALMON WITH SALSA
STRAWBERRIES, GRAND MARNIER
& WHITE CHOCOLATE

MONTEREY:
THE ROMANTIC HUB

THE FIRST TOURIST visited Monterey in 1602, when Sebastiano Vizcaino of Spain sailed into Monterey Bay. And the visitors have just kept coming to the romantic hub of the Monterey Peninsula.

By 1770, six years before the Declaration of Independence was signed, Monterey was declared the capital of Alta California. That makes Monterey older than the United States.

Since that time, the city has survived pirates, naval attacks, bandits, duels in the streets, tales of sea serpents, and suitors serenading their sweethearts in secluded patios.

AND THROUGH it all, Monterey has carefully nurtured a reputation for fine cooking. The availability of a wide variety of fresh seafood and easy access to fertile fields and vineyards insure that the tradition is maintained.

Wander through the jumble of downtown streets and you will understand that the streets were set up to follow meandering cowpaths. And, like the twisting cowpaths, Monterey's history is mixed with legend, mystery and charm.

1815 poster for fight to the death between a grizzly bear and a bull.

FOR EXAMPLE, the Memory Garden, a walled yard at the Pacific House is a tranquil spot to sit and enjoy the old fountain's water lilies and well-tended flowers. But this was also the spot where an early California form of entertainment took place. Grizzly bears and bulls, each with a leg tied to a single rope, fought to the death to the cheers of the crowd.

California's First Theater, dating from 1847, still offers theatrical productions. The first show packed the 150-seat house at $5 per ticket. You'll recognize the theater—it's the one with whale ribs on the front porch.

The Old Whaling Station, built in 1847, is a lovely two-story house with manicured gardens. At one time, it was headquarters for a company of Portuguese whalers, complete with a front walk made of whalebone. Next door is the first brick building erected in California. The owner left Monterey as soon as gold was discovered in the Sierras.

THE FIRST constitution of California was signed in 1849 in Colton Hall. The hall, now a museum adjacent to the city's municipal center, houses memorabilia of that historic time. In counterpoint to the origins of Colton Hall, a redwood tree in front of the graceful edifice was grown from seeds that were carried to the moon by astronauts.

MANY OF the graceful adobe structures of the old days are preserved to this day. Many are still in use, others are preserved as historic monuments and are open to tours.

Cannery Row was immortalized by author John Steinbeck. The sardine canneries have been converted to other uses or have been torn down. But some of the places featured in his books still remain: Doc Ricketts' Lab is a private club; Lee Chong's grocery store now sells souvenirs, and the Hovden Cannery has been completely rebuilt to house the Monterey Bay Aquarium.

A wealth of salmon and sardines formed the backbone of Monterey's economy for much of this century. In 1918, there were nine canneries along the waterfront. By 1945, there were 19 canneries operating full-bore. In some years 230,000 tons of sardines were canned or reduced for fish meal and oil.

In 1945, the sardines began to disappear. By 1950, what had been the greatest sardine port in the world was virtually a ghost port in the fishing industry. The rusting remains served as a setting for some of Steinbeck's most famous novels.

SOME OF THE history and lore of those hectic days is preserved at the Monterey Bay Aquarium, a $50 million facility that specializes in the critters of Monterey Bay and their habitats. One of the few aquariums that specializes in indigenous critters, the huge facility houses thousands of specimens.

Attractions at the aquarium include a sea otter tank complete with private beach for the playful mammals, bat rays you can pet, a trout stream, a user-friendly tide pool, and a unique kelp forest in the world's tallest tank.

Fisherman's Wharf is the descendant of a series of Monterey wharves dating back to 1845. Accompanied by an ever-present chorus of barking sea lions, visitors browse through specialty shops, seafood markets and restaurants and catch rides on tour boats when the whales migrate past the Monterey shore. A nearby wharf, built in 1925, serves as a cargo pier and contains facilities for the commercial fishing industry.

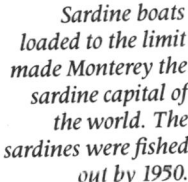

Sardine boats loaded to the limit made Monterey the sardine capital of the world. The sardines were fished out by 1950.

MONTEREY DATEBOOK: Monterey Film Festival, February; Adobe Tour, April; Squid Festival, May; Monterey Triple Crown, at Laguna Seca Raceway, May; Merienda (Monterey's birthday party), June; The Blues Festival, June; Monterey National Horse Show, July; Obon Festival, July; Santa Rosalia Festival (blessing of the fleet), September; Monterey Jazz Festival, September; California Wine Festival, November; Posada Procession and Piñata Party, December.

THE JABBERWOCK

598 Laine Street
Monterey, CA 93940
(408)372-4777
Rooms $100–$175

THE JABBERWOCK bed and breakfast, a 7 room post-Victorian home, is 4 blocks above Cannery Row and the Monterey Bay Aquarium. It's hidden behind an ivy wall in a quiet neighborhood. And when you pass through, you've entered Alice's Wonderland, finding ½-acre estate gardens with waterfalls overlooking Monterey Bay.

With spacious public areas and enclosed sunporch where you may enjoy an array of hors d'oeuvres and sherry each evening, you can relax looking at the sailboats. Each room is appointed with antique or period furniture, down pillows and comforters and before bedtime, cookies and milk await you.

Every morning you awake to the fresh aroma of a home-made breakfast. And when you have to leave, you will truly know that you have passed "through the Looking Glass."

Caviar and Stuff

Preparation Time: 5 Minutes

½ lb. cream cheese room temperature
½ small onion finely chopped
 1 small jar red caviar (1¾ oz. jar)
2-3 tsps. cream

Soften the cream cheese in a mixer, adding cream and onions. Gently fold in caviar. Serve with watercrackers.

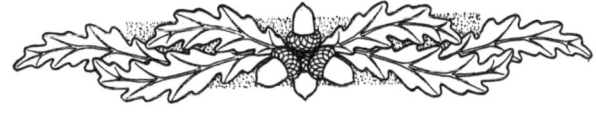

Artichokes and Stuff

Preparation Time: 15 Minutes

 1 can artichokes, drained
 1 cup sour cream
½ tsp. beef bouillon crystals
 2 Tbsps. sesame seed oil
¼ cup chopped fresh dill

Quarter the artichokes and set aside. Combine last four ingredients and let stand at least 10 minutes for bouillon to dissolve. Fold in artichokes. Serve with crackers.

OLD MONTEREY INN

500 Martin Street
Monterey, CA 93940
(408)375-8284
Rooms $160–$220

An ARCHITECTURAL GEM in a forest-like setting, the Old Monterey Inn is a charming English country house with a unique sense of history and romance. The handsome half-timbered house sits on an oak-studded hillside in a quiet residential neighborhood, surrounded by more than an acre of beautifully landscaped gardens.

All 10 delightful rooms have private baths, and most feature wood-burning fireplaces, skylights and stained-glass windows. Each room is individually designed to be a romantic delight.

Complimentary breakfast, decanted sherry, fresh flowers and fruit, plus afternoon wine and cheese create a unique experience for the discriminating guest.

Scones

Preparation Time: 45 Minutes
Pre-heat oven to 350°
Yields: 15 scones

3 cups white flour
4 tsps. baking powder
   Dash of salt
½ cube butter, cut into 4
   pieces

2 eggs
½ pt. whipping cream
¾ cup raisins or currants

In a food processor blend flour, baking powder, salt and butter. Transfer the mixture into a large bowl and blend eggs, whipping cream and raisins. (If dough is too dry to hold together, add a little water).

Gently roll the dough into a ball and place on a floured surface. Roll to ¾ inch thickness. Use a 2-inch cookie cutter and cut into 15 scones. Save ¼ cup egg and cream mixture, add a little sugar and brush tops. Bake at 350°, 20-30 minutes.

Serve with butter and jam.

Fruit Soup

Preparation Time: 25 Minutes
Serves 8

½ cup coarse-cut seeded
   watermelon
½ cup strawberries
½ cup coarse-cut peaches
1 cup bananas
1 cup apple juice

1 cup cranberry juice
½ cup orange juice
½ cup lemon or lime juice
½ cup wine or champagne
   (optional)
Fresh mint leaves

Combine the first 9 ingredients in a blender, to make your stock. Add the following cut fruit: ½ cup each, strawberry halves, watermelon chunks, seedless grapes, peach slices, pineapple chunks, cantaloupe balls and honeydew balls.

The soup can be served at room temperature or cold. Flavors improve the longer the soup sits.

CAFE FINA

ITALIAN CUISINE
47 Fisherman's Wharf
Monterey
372-5200
Lunch and dinner daily from 11:30AM
AVERAGE DINNER FOR TWO: $30

GENEROUS PORTIONS OF fresh seafood, mesquite-grilled chicken and beef are featured in this delightful wharfside restaurant. Specialties include brick oven pizzettes smothered with fresh tomato sauces, assorted cheeses and toppings ranging from salmon to sausage.

The handmade pastas and ravioli are legendary and are served either with red or white sauces and flavored with fresh garden herbs. A complete wine list features California and Italian wines in addition to a full bar.

Located on historic Fisherman's Wharf, the setting is ideal. Foghorns, ships' bells, and seagulls fill the air with sound, and often, as dinner begins, the setting sun floods the dining room with light.

Menu for Four

Oysters Rockefeller
Lentil Soup
Cabbage Salad with Radicchio & Prosciutto
Fina Pasta
Raspberry Granita

Oysters Rockefeller

Serves 4
Preparation Time: 45 Minutes
Pre-heat oven to 500°

24 live oysters
½ lb. bacon
2 large onions
1 Tbsp. brandy
4 bunches spinach, cleaned
4 cups rock salt
Hollandaise sauce, optional

Open the oysters, remove meat with juice and set aside. Save the bottom half of each oyster shell and clean with warm water. Do not use soap.

In a large sauté pan, cook bacon until brown, about 8 minutes. Add onion and continue cooking until browned, about 15 minutes. Add brandy. This will cause a flame. Let some of the alcohol burn off, then cover pan and remove from heat and cool.

In a large pot, bring enough salted water to boil to cover four bunches of spinach. Cook for 5 minutes, drain well and cool.

With a food processor, mix and chop the spinach, bacon, onion, oysters and reserved juice. Place a spoonful of this mixture in each of the cleaned oyster shells. Place filled oyster shells in oven for 10 minutes or until hot.

Serve oysters on a bed of rock salt. You may wish to top each oyster with your favorite hollandaise sauce.

Lentil Soup

Serves 4
Preparation Time: 1½ Hours (note soaking time)

1 **cup dry lentils**
6 **cups water**
1 **cup tomatoes, peeled**
2 **cups celery, chopped**
2 **cups onion, chopped**
1 **cup carrots, chopped**
2 **bay leaves**
1 **tsp. dried basil**
1 **pinch dried thyme**
1 **tsp. garlic, chopped**
3 **Tbsps. olive oil**
  Salt and pepper to taste

Soak lentils in tap water for 45 minutes, then drain.

Bring 6 cups of water to a boil and add the presoaked lentils. Cook until lentils are soft, about 30 minutes. Add tomatoes, lower heat and simmer.

Add celery, onions, carrots, herbs and garlic and continue cooking over low heat for 30 minutes or until desired texture.

Before serving, add olive oil, salt and pepper.

Cabbage Salad with Radicchio & Prosciutto Ham

Preparation Time: 15 Minutes

 1 small head cabbage
 1 head radicchio
 ¼ lb. prosciutto, thinly sliced
 ¼ cup walnuts, chopped

Slice the head of cabbage in half, lengthwise. Remove most of the core. Slice cabbage thinly crosswise. Do the same with radicchio.

Place cabbage and radicchio in bowl with prosciutto and chopped walnuts. Refrigerate until ready to serve.

Vinaigrette

 ½ cup walnut oil
 4 Tbsps. olive oil
 3 Tbsps. raspberry vinegar
 Oregano, basil, garlic, salt and pepper to taste

Combine all ingredients in a jar and shake well. Serve over salad.

Fina Pasta

Serves 4

Preparation Time: 30 Minutes

½ lb. butter
1 lb. shrimp, cooked, peeled
1 lb. Roma tomatoes, chopped
½ cup black olives, sliced
½ cup green onions, chopped
½ cup clam juice
1 Tbsp. shallots, minced
Dash of cayenne pepper
½ lb. linguine pasta

In a large sauté pan, melt butter over medium heat. Add the shrimp, tomatoes, olives, onions and clam juice, stirring constantly until hot. Add the shallots and pepper, remove from heat.

Bring a large pot of salted water to a boil. Cook the linguine in the boiling water until al dente.

Drain and return to the pan. Immediately stir in the Fina sauce and serve.

Raspberry Granita

Preparation Time: 35 Minutes

2 packages pectin
6 baskets fresh raspberries
½ cup lemon juice
6 Tbsps. raspberry liqueur
4 cups sugar

Dissolve the pectin in water according to directions. Place all the ingredients in one-gallon ice cream machine. Add water to ⅔ capacity. Run machine for 20 to 30 minutes.

DOMENICO'S ON THE WHARF RESTAURANT

SEAFOOD/ITALIAN CUISINE
50 Fisherman's Wharf
Monterey, CA 93940
372-3655
Lunch Monday–Saturday 11:30AM–2:30PM
Lunch Sunday 11:30AM to 3PM
Dinner Monday–Friday 5PM until closing
Dinner Saturday–Sunday 4PM until closing
AVERAGE DINNER FOR TWO: $40

DOMENICO'S IS AN elegant, lively and eclectic seafood restaurant on Fisherman's Wharf, specializing in Italian cuisine.

While waiting for a table, it's fun to mingle with the lively crowd at the oyster bar and sip a glass of wine from the large cellar of imported and domestic wines.

For dining with a view, tables are set along the windows the length of the dining room. Guests enjoy a never-ending water show of strutting sea gulls, diving pelicans, cavorting harbor seals and an occasional sea otter with its catch of the day, all set against the backdrop of Monterey's historic harbor and fishing fleet.

Menu for Four

Tomato-Ginger Soup
Marinated Scallops
Seafood Pasta

Tomato-Ginger Soup

Serves 4
Preparation Time: 45 Minutes

2½ oz. ginger, peeled and sliced
  1 medium onion coarsely chopped
  2 lbs. plum tomatoes, peeled, seeded, chopped
  4 Tbsps. unsalted butter
1¼ cups chicken stock
  1 Tbsp. sugar
    Salt and pepper to taste
¾ cup cream
  2 egg yolks
    Watercress leaves for garnish

In a food processor, puree the onion and ginger until smooth. Transfer the mixture to a bowl. Add the tomatoes to the food processor, puree until smooth; set aside.

Melt the butter over medium heat in a large heavy saucepan. Add the onion puree and cook, stirring frequently, until the mixture begins to color, about 5 minutes. Add the tomato puree, chicken stock, sugar, salt and pepper. Bring the mixture to a boil, stirring occasionally. Add the cream, reduce the heat to low and simmer uncovered for 30 minutes. Taste the soup and add more sugar if necessary, to balance the acidity of the tomatoes.

Beat the egg yolks with a whisk to blend. Add the mixture to the saucepan and stir over medium-low heat until the soup thickens, about 2 minutes. Do not allow the soup to boil. Strain the soup through a fine sieve into a clean saucepan. If the soup is to sit any length of time, place a piece of plastic wrap directly against the surface to prevent a skin from forming.

Garnish with watercress leaves.

Marinated Scallops

Serves 4
Preparation Time: 15 Minutes (note refrigeration time)

1 lb. fresh scallops (20-30 count)
½ cup water chestnuts sliced thin
1 leek diced (white part only)
5 mushrooms sliced
1 Tbsp. shredded red ginger
1 Tbsp. soy sauce
1 Tbsp. honey
1 tsp. rice vinegar
1 tsp. sesame seed oil
1 Tbsp. olive oil
Juice of ½ lime
1 garlic clove, minced
2 dashes of Tabasco
Black pepper to taste

Cook scallops in boiling, lightly salted water 5-7 minutes. Remove from heat, cool with cold water.

Mix the above ingredients together. Add the scallops. Marinade for 2 to 3 hours before serving.

Seafood Pasta

Serves 4
Preparation Time: 20 Minutes

12 large shrimp
16 littleneck clams
16 mussels
16 shucked oysters
 8 oz. fresh scallops
 8 oz. squid
 5 garlic cloves, minced
 5 shallots, minced
¾ cup butter
 4 cups marinara sauce
 4 oz. white wine
1½ cups clam juice
   Lemon and parsley garnish
 1 lb. cooked linguine

In a heavy sauce pot cook the shrimp lightly on both sides in butter. Add all ingredients except the squid. Cook for 5 minutes, then add squid and cover pot, until clams and mussels open.

Serve over fresh linguine. Garnish with lemon crowns and sprinkle with chopped parsley.

EPSILON

GREEK CUISINE
422 Tyler Street
Monterey
655-8108
Lunch Monday–Friday 11 AM–2:30PM
Dinner Tuesday–Saturday 5PM–9PM
Closed Sunday
AVERAGE DINNER FOR TWO: $25

EPSILON OFFERS A warm, friendly, casual atmosphere, good service and exceptional food. The menu features traditional Greek and Mediterranean specialties that are consistently fresh and delicious.

This restaurant has become so popular that it expanded by annexing a small space next door. The high-ceilinged contemporary dining room is gaily painted and well decorated with Greek art work.

On top of all this good cooking, generous portions, and very reasonable prices, patrons are treated so warmly at Epsilon that they want to come back again and again.

Epsilon
Fine Greek Food

Menu for Four

Country Greek Salad
Chicken Soup with Egg Lemon Sauce
Spanakopita
Almond Baklava

Country Greek Salad

Serves 4
Preparation Time: 20 Minutes

- **3 tomatoes**
- **2 cucumbers**
- **1 head green leaf lettuce**
- **1 red onion, diced**
- **1 small green pepper, chopped fine**
- **2 Tbsps. capers, optional**
- **Kalamata olives**
- **¼ cup virgin olive oil**
- **3 Tbsps. red wine vinegar**
- **Salt and pepper to taste**
- **Dash of oregano**
- **7 oz. Greek feta cheese**

Slice the tomatoes and cucumbers into small pieces.

Tear or finely chop the lettuce.

In a salad bowl, combine the tomatoes, cucumbers, lettuce, onion, peppers, capers and olives.

In a small mixing bowl, whisk together the olive oil, vinegar, salt, pepper and oregano. Pour the dressing over the salad and toss well.

Top salad with crumbled feta cheese before serving.

Chicken Soup
with Egg Lemon Sauce

Serves 4
Preparation Time: 1½ Hours

1 large chicken
2 lemons
3 Tbsps. olive oil
1 carrot, chopped
1 yellow onion, chopped
2 ribs of celery, chopped
2 bay leaves
5 cloves
8 black peppercorns
½ gal. water
½ cup rice
3 large eggs
¼ bunch of parsley, chopped

Skin and wash the chicken, then rub it with the peel of 2 lemons. Reserve the lemons. Place chicken in a stock pot with the olive oil and brown over medium heat for 4 to 5 minutes.

Add the carrots, onion, celery, bay leaves, cloves and peppercorns and sauté for 2 minutes. Add the water, bringing the soup to a boil. Cover and simmer for about 45 minutes or until the chicken is cooked through.

Remove the chicken and strain the broth. Return the broth to the stock pot and bring to a boil over medium heat. Add the rice and continue to cook for 20 minutes. Remove from heat.

Cut the chicken meat into small pieces. Set aside.

Beat the eggs and juice of 2 lemons together very slowly. Gently stir in the egg-lemon mixture, in small batches, into the broth. Add the diced chicken meat and sprinkle with chopped parsley.

Spanakopita

Serves 4
Preparation Time: 1 Hour
Pre-heat oven to 350°

1 onion, finely chopped
2 Tbsps. extra virgin olive oil
2 bunches fresh spinach, cleaned, dried
2 eggs, beaten
   Salt and pepper to taste
2 Tbsps. fresh dill, finely chopped
1 cup feta cheese, crumbled
8 sheets phyllo dough
¼ cup melted butter

Sauté the onions in olive oil over medium heat until they become transparent but not brown. Add the spinach and eggs and cook until tender. Season to taste with salt and pepper. Reduce heat to low and cook for about 15 minutes. Add the dill and the feta cheese. Set aside.

Unroll the phyllo and place several sheets in an oiled pie pan, brushing each sheet lightly with the melted butter. Place the spinach mixture in the pan and top with more phyllo dough. Brush the top with butter. Before baking, cut the pie into serving size pieces.

Bake at 350° for 40 to 50 minutes or until the phyllo is golden brown on top.

Almond Baklava

Serves 4
Preparation Time: 1¾ Hours
Pre-heat oven to 350°

3 cups almonds, toasted, finely chopped
¼ cup sugar
1 Tbsp. cinnamon
1 lb. phyllo dough
½ cup butter, melted

In a mixing bowl, combine the almonds, sugar and cinnamon.

Using a pastry brush or a small paint brush, butter a baking sheet. Unroll the phyllo dough. Carefully place two sheets of phyllo on the baking sheet. They should be flat and unwrinkled. Brush the top with butter and sprinkle with chopped almonds. Work quickly or keep the remaining unbuttered phyllo dough covered or it will dry and crack and become difficult to use. Continue this procedure until about half of the phyllo is used.

Repeat the procedure, making successive layers of equal thickness. Finish with a thicker layer of phyllo sheets (6 to 8 sheets), brushing each sheet lightly with butter.

With a sharp knife, score the baklava into diamond shaped pieces. Sprinkle with water and bake at 350° for 45 minutes to 1 hour or until golden brown.

Remove from the oven and immediately pour the syrup (recipe follows) over the baklava. Allow to cool for 30 minutes to absorb the syrup before serving.

Baklava Syrup

1 cup honey
½ cup sugar
⅓ cup water
1 cinnamon stick, optional
8 cloves
   Juice of ½ lemon

In a saucepan, over medium heat, combine the honey, sugar, water, cinnamon stick and cloves, bringing the mixture to a boil for about 15 minutes or until the syrup becomes thickened.

Remove from heat and add lemon juice.

Allow syrup to cool before pouring over the baklava.

FERRANTE'S RESTAURANT

ITALIAN CUISINE
MONTEREY MARRIOTT
350 Calle Principal
Monterey
649-4234
Dinner nightly 5PM–11PM
Sunday brunch 10AM–2PM
AVERAGE DINNER FOR TWO: $50

THE LOCATION COULD not be more ideal. Across the street from Fisherman's Wharf and a scenic 30-minute stroll to Cannery Row and the Monterey Bay Aquarium is the Monterey Marriott.

Ferrante's sits atop the hotel like an eagle's nest, offering gourmet Italian country-style cuisine along with unparalleled views. Exciting specialties, late night menu, elegant Sunday brunches and full bar make this restaurant a local favorite.

The Marriott also includes 344 guest rooms, a fully equipped health club, sauna, hot tub, heated outdoor pool and Marriott service second to none.

Menu for Six

Cream of Zucchini Soup
Stuffed Mushrooms
Fettucine Ferrante's

Cream of Zucchini Soup

Serves 6
Preparation Time: 25 Minutes

5 medium zucchini
1 medium onion
¼ lb. butter
1 qt. chicken stock
¼ cup flour
½ cup cream
   Italian seasonings to taste
4 Tbsps. Parmesan cheese
6 sprigs of parsley, chopped

Sauté the shredded zucchini and diced onions with butter until tender. Add the flour, chicken stock and seasoning. Stir and simmer until the soup is quite thick. Add the cream.

When serving, top with Parmesan and parsley garnish.

Stuffed Mushrooms

Serves 6
Preparation Time: 15 Minutes

12 large mushroom caps
½ lb. prosciutto, julienned
2 Tbsps. dried oregano
2 cups mozzarella, grated
1 Tbsp. Parmesan, grated
2 tsps. garlic, pureed
1 Tbsp. parsley, chopped
  Black pepper to taste
  Lemon

Remove the mushroom stems and steam the caps (slightly crispy).

Mix all ingredients together in a medium mixing bowl, by hand. Making small balls from the mixture, stuff into cooked mushrooms caps.

Place the caps on a plate, in a circle, and top with a little Parmesan cheese. Brown under the broiler.

Place on a lined plate and serve hot, with fresh lemon.

Fettucine Ferrante's

Serves 6
Preparation Time: 20 Minutes

28 oz. egg fettucine
4 cups chicken breast, julienned
1 head broccoli
1 cup cashews
1 cup Parmesan, grated
3 cups heavy cream
1 clove garlic, chopped
Salt and pepper to taste

Cook the egg fettucine al dente and set aside.

Sauté the chicken in a medium sauté pan to brown. Add the garlic, broccoli, seasonings and cream. Let the cream reduce on medium heat for 3 minutes. Add the cashews and fettucine.

Sprinkle with Parmesan cheese before serving.

THE FISHERY RESTAURANT

SEAFOOD/ASIAN CUISINE
21 Soledad Drive
Monterey, CA 93940
373-6200
Dinner Tuesday–Saturday 5PM–9PM
AVERAGE DINNER FOR TWO: $30

THE FISHERY IS noted for its international cuisine and Asian specialties featuring a large selection of fresh seafood and a most extraordinary salad bar.

Owners Jerry Meyer and Glen Blanchar have traveled extensively throughout the Orient to sharpen their culinary skills and bring home many innovative recipes.

A cozy and inviting atmosphere where you can relax and enjoy your evening meal.

Mobil Travel Award winner.

Curried Squid Cocktail
Crispy Fish in Sweet and Sour Sauce
Nutcracker Flambé

Curried Squid Cocktail

Serves 4
Preparation Time: 15 Minutes

2 lbs. squid filets cleaned
6 Tbsps. mayonnaise
1 Tbsp. curry powder
1 cup green onions, chopped
1 cup celery, chopped
1 tsp. salt
Garnish with lettuce and tomatoes

Dip squid filets into rapidly boiling water. Cook for 2 minutes. Drain. Rinse with cold water and chop into bite-size pieces.

Mix together remaining ingredients and toss squid bits into mixture. Chill thoroughly.

Serve on a bed of finely chopped lettuce and chilled tomatoes.

Crispy Fish in Sweet and Sour Sauce

Serves 4
Preparation Time: 25 Minutes

Eight 10 oz. white fish fillets
2 Tbsps. light soy sauce
¼ tsp. salt
½ tsp. sesame oil
¼ tsp. ginger juice
1 Tbsp. water
3 cups plus 2 Tbsps. oil
1 cup flour
4 Tbsps. cornstarch
1½ tsps. baking powder
1 tsp. garlic, chopped
Garnish with shredded lettuce

Cut fish filets into 1-inch cubes. Marinate in soy sauce, salt, sesame oil, ginger juice, water and 1 Tbsp. oil, and let stand for 10 minutes.

Heat the wok and add 3 cups of oil. Combine the flour, cornstarch, baking powder and 1 Tbsp. oil for batter. Add enough water to make the mixture runny. Dip the fish in the batter and deep fry in hot oil until golden brown. Drain and remove to a plate with slotted spoon and set aside.

Heat 1 tsp. oil to stir fry garlic. Add sweet and sour sauce and bring to a boil.

To serve, garnish the fish cubes with shredded lettuce and serve sweet and sour sauce as dip.

Sweet and Sour Sauce

Combine ¾ cup water, 3 Tbsps. tomato sauce, 1 Tbsp. tomato puree, 2 Tbsps. vinegar, 3 Tbsps. sugar, 1 Tbsp. cornstarch, 1 chicken bouillon cube, ¼ tsp. sesame oil and 1 tsp. red chile. Mix well.

Nutcracker Flambé

Serves 4
Preparation Time: 5 Minutes

1 cup macadamia nuts, chopped
5 Tbsps. butter
5 Tbsps. brown sugar
1 Tbsp. Amaretto
1 qt. French vanilla ice cream

Combine the nuts, butter and brown sugar in a saucepan over medium heat. Flambé with the Amaretto. Stir until the mixture is foamy and hot.

Pour over the ice cream until caramelized.

FRESH CREAM RESTAURANT

FRENCH CUISINE
Heritage Harbor
99 Pacific Street
Monterey
375-9798
Dinner nightly from 6PM
AVERAGE DINNER FOR TWO: $70

FRESH CREAM RESTAURANT creates an elegant mood, with a menu to match. This award-winning restaurant is noted for its distinctive classical French cuisine with a California flair.

An ever-changing menu combines seasonal fresh ingredients, featuring such house specialties as roast boned duck in black currant sauce, rack of lamb Dijonnaise and Grand Marnier soufflé.

Fresh Cream is a place for unhurried dining and quiet conversation in an intimate atmosphere.

Menu for Six

Mixed Greens with Balsamic Vinaigrette
Lobster Ravioli
Chocolate Bag with Ice Cream Shake

Mixed Greens with Balsamic Vinaigrette

Serves 6
Preparation Time: 10 Minutes

 1 Tbsp. garlic, minced
 1 Tbsp. shallots, minced
 1 Tbsp. Dijon mustard
 ¼ bunch chives, sliced thin
 3 stems, parsley, chopped
 1½ cups balsamic vinegar
   Salt and pepper to taste
 2 cups olive oil
 6 cups mixed salad greens

In a large mixing bowl, combine the garlic, shallots, mustard, chives, parsley and vinegar. Season with salt and pepper.

Whisk in the olive oil, until emulsified. Serve at room temperature, refrigerating between uses.

Gently toss the mixed salad greens with the dressing before serving.

Lobster Ravioli

Serves 6
Preparation Time: 45 Minutes (note dough time)

3 eggs
1 cup Semolina flour
1 cup all-purpose flour
2 Tbsps. olive oil
¼ tsp. salt
½ lb. tiger shrimp, peeled, deveined
1 lb. lobster meat

1 Tbsp. cognac
2 egg whites
Fresh ground pepper to taste
¾ cups heavy cream
Egg wash (mix 1 egg and 1 Tbsp. water)

In a food processor, blend the eggs, flour, olive oil and salt. Remove and knead by hand until the dough is elastic and smooth. Let rest, covered, for 3 hours.

Prepare the filling by combining the shrimp, lobster, cognac, egg whites and pepper in a food processor or blender. Lightly blend to rough consistency before adding the cream.

Roll the dough into two thin sheets. On one sheet of dough, place small mounds of the filling and egg wash edges around each filling. Place the second sheet of dough over the first and press with edge of palm to seal layers together. Use any type of cutting utensil you wish. Place on parchment paper and refrigerate until use.

Before serving, bring a pot of water to a simmer, never a boil, adding a small amount of oil. Cook the ravioli for 5 minutes. Serve immediately.

Lobster Sauce

Preparation Time: 20 Minutes

1½ qt. lobster stock
3 Tbsps. tomato puree

3 Tbsps. cognac
Unsalted butter

Combine the lobster stock, tomato puree and the cognac in a large sauce pot over medium heat, reducing to a thick soup consistency.

Put sauce into blender and cover. Turn on medium speed, adding soft unsalted butter until desired thickness.

Pour over lobster ravioli and serve.

Chocolate Bag with Ice Cream Shake

Serves 6
Preparation Time: 20 Minutes (note refrigeration time)

2 lbs. chocolate
6 small coffee bags with wax liners
1 qt. espresso ice cream
  Heavy cream

In a sauce pan over low heat, melt your favorite chocolate, we use suisse tobamera. Remove from heat.

With a small paint brush paint the inside of each coffee bag with the melted chocolate. You can add up to four layers of chocolate, as desired, by refrigerating between each painted layer.

In a blender combine the ice cream with a heavy cream until desired thickness is achieved. Pour the ice cream shake into the chocolate bag and serve.

Portola Cafe

MONTEREY BAY AQUARIUM
CALIFORNIA CUISINE
886 Cannery Row
Monterey
648-4870
Cafeteria daily 10AM–5PM daily
Dining room 11AM–3PM daily
AVERAGE DINNER FOR TWO: $30

ALL THE WONDERS of a hidden world come to light at the internationally acclaimed Monterey Bay Aquarium. Nearly 100 innovative habitat galleries and exhibits plunge you into Monterey Bay on a journey to its deep reefs, rocky shores and turbulent tide pools. The aquarium puts you eye-to-eye with more than 6,000 strange and colorful creatures that call Monterey Bay home, from playful sea otters to graceful sharks, elusive octopus and fierce wolf-eels.

The Monterey Bay Aquarium also houses the Portola Cafe, a 50-seat restaurant located at the west end of historic Cannery Row. The restaurant offers spectacular bay views and two dining options: a self-service buffet or full-service luncheons. The Portola Cafe offers a unique setting to enjoy outstanding California fare and watch the activities on the bay.

Menu for Four

Crab and Seafood Cakes
Roasted Garlic and Corn Flan
with Red Bell Pepper Sauce
Fresh Berry Tarts with Pastry Cream

Crab and Seafood Cakes

Serves 4
Preparation Time: 45 Minutes

½ loaf sourdough bread
¼ lb. sea scallops
1 Tbsp. flour
1 egg
½ cup cream
¼ lb. crab meat
¼ lb. salmon, cut in small cubes
¼ lb. snapper, cut in small cubes

2 small scallions, sliced thin
2 Tbsps. red pimento, diced small
½ tsp. salt
Dash of cayenne pepper
¼ cup vegetable oil
Tomatoes, diced as garnish
Chives, diced as garnish

Trim the crust from the bread and pulse in a food processor until bread becomes fine crumbs. Remove and reserve until later.

Add scallops to the food processor and run on high for 1 minute before adding the flour and egg. Return to high for 1 minute and slowly add the cream until it is fully incorporated into the scallop mixture. Place this mixture into a bowl and fold in the remaining ingredients, except the oil and bread crumbs.

Scoop 8 individual tablespoons of the seafood mixture and roll in the bread crumbs to coat thoroughly. Place on a flat surface and gently press into small circles approximately ½" high. Sauté in oil until golden brown. Remove from heat and drain on paper towels.

To serve, place the flan (recipe on following page) on top of the plate with 4 tablespoons of red bell pepper sauce in the center. Place 2 crab cakes on top of the sauce and garnish with chives and diced tomatoes.

Roasted Garlic and Corn Flan

Serves 4
Preparation Time: 1 Hour
Pre-heat oven to 250°

  6 **large garlic cloves**
  1 **Tbsp. olive oil**
  1 **Tbsp. corn starch**
  2 **eggs**
  1 **egg yolk**
  1 **pt. half and half**
  1 **ear of corn, about ½ cup**
    Salt and white pepper to taste

    Peel garlic and toss lightly in olive oil. In a baking dish, place the garlic and corn, with the husk on, in oven. Roast the corn for 10 minutes or until cooked slightly. Roast the garlic for 5–10 minutes longer, or until soft. Remove the corn kernels from the husk and combine with the roasted garlic. Add the corn starch, eggs, salt and pepper.

    Warm the half and half over low heat to 160°. Slowly pour into the garlic mixture, stirring constantly. Pour the flan into a small, lightly buttered oven-proof containers, approximately ¼ cup each, and place in a water bath. Bake at 250° for 20–25 minutes. Cool and turn out.

Red Bell Pepper Sauce

Pre-heat oven to 500°

  1 **large red bell pepper**
  1 **Tbsp. olive oil**
  4 **Tbsps. mayonnaise**
  1 **Tbsp. red wine vinegar**
 ½ **tsp. sugar**
    Salt and white pepper

    Lightly coat the pepper with oil and place in a very hot oven until the skin begins to blister. Remove and wrap in plastic to cool. When cool, peel and seed the pepper and place into a blender with the remaining ingredients. Purée to desired consistency.

Fresh Berry Tarts

Serves 4
Preparation Time: 30 Minutes
Pre-heat oven to 350°

½ lb. pie dough
  Dry beans
  Pastry cream, recipe follows
8 strawberries, sliced
12 blackberries

12 raspberries
½ cup whipped cream
2 Tbsps. sugar
1 small piece vanilla bean
4 sprigs of mint

Roll pie dough to ¼" and line 4 tart molds. Fill molds with dry beans and cook until done, about 15 minutes. Remove beans and let dough cool.

Spread 2 Tbsps. of the pastry cream in each tart. Arrange strawberry slices around the outer crust with raspberries and blueberries inside the tart.

Whip the cream, sugar and vanilla to stiff peaks. Place one spoonful in the center of the berries and garnish with mint.

Pastry Cream

1 qt. milk
1 tsp. vanilla extract
4 Tbsps. cornstarch

1 cup sugar
4 eggs
Pinch of salt

In a large saucepan, heat the milk and vanilla until just boiling.

Meanwhile, in a large mixing bowl combine the cornstarch and sugar, gradually adding the eggs. Mix until smooth. Add ⅓ of the hot milk to the egg mixture, whisking constantly.

Add the egg mixture back into the remaining hot milk, adding the salt, and cooking over medium heat, stirring constantly with a wooden spoon until thick. If the cream burns when thickening, you can save the flavor by straining the cream.

SARDINE FACTORY RESTAURANT

ITALIAN CUISINE
701 Wave Street
Monterey, CA 93940
373-3775
Dinner nightly from 4PM
AVERAGE DINNER FOR TWO: $65

THE SARDINE FACTORY, a popular and unique restaurant located at historic Cannery Row, is world renowned for its excellent cuisine, extensive wine list and impeccable service.

The cocktail lounge contains a 120-year-old hand-carved bar, and displayed on the walls is a pictorial history of Cannery Row. In addition to the original dining room, there are four other distinctive dining areas.

Ted Balestreri and Bert Cutino opened the Sardine Factory in 1968, and since that time have received numerous awards.

The Sardine Factory, with its warm and friendly atmosphere, superb service and excellent menu, offers the ultimate opportunity for elegant dining.

Menu for Four

Calamari Fritters
Escargot en Toscani
Prawns Baltino
Prawns Sambucca
Swordfish Steak with Sundried Tomato Tapenade
Osso Buco
Apple Filled Purse with Creme Anglaise

Calamari Fritters

Serves 4
Preparation Time: 25 Minutes (note refrigeration time)

> 2 lbs. squid, cleaned
> 1 onion, chopped
> 1 egg, beaten
> 1 tsp. parsley, chopped
> ¼ cup green onions, chopped
> ½ Tbsps. garlic, granulated
>   Salt and pepper to taste
> ¼ cup bread crumbs
> ¼ cup fine cracker meal
> 2 cups corn oil

Chop the cleaned squid into bite-size pieces. In a large mixing bowl, combine the calamari with the onion, egg, parley, green onions and garlic, blending well. Season with salt and pepper. Add the bread crumbs and stir well to combine.

Shape the mixture into 2 oz.-size oval balls and roll in the cracker meal. Place on wax paper and let set in the refrigerator for 1 hour.

Heat the oil in a large skillet. When it is very hot, fry the calamari in the oil until brown and crispy. Drain on paper towels before serving hot.

Escargot en Toscani

Serves 4
Preparation Time: 30 Minutes
Pre-heat oven to 400°

 2 each Toscani bread or French baguette
24 large French snails
24 Tbsps. (3 sticks) butter
 2 Tbsps. garlic, chopped
 2 Tbsps. Pernod
 2 Tbsps. lemon juice
½ cup parsley, chopped
 2 tsps. salt
 2 tsps. white pepper
 1 cup heavy cream
   Parsley sprigs for garnish

Slice bread into 2" lengths. Partially hollow out the bread pieces and fill with the escargot.

Place butter in a mixing bowl and process at high speed with an electric mixer until the butter is whipped. Slowly, add the garlic, Pernod, lemon juice, parsley, salt and pepper, carefully mixing together all the ingredients.

Place 1 tsp. of the butter mixture on top of each snail to seal it in the bread pocket.

Bake the snails at 400° for 10 minutes.

In a heavy saucepan, combine the cream and remaining butter mixture over medium-high heat until the sauce thickens.

To serve, arrange 6 escargots on each plate and drizzle with sauce. Garnish with fresh parsley sprigs.

Prawns Baltino

Serves 4
Preparation Time: 30 Minutes

24 **large prawns**
 4 **Tbps. olive oil**
 1 **tsp. shallots, chopped fine**
 1 **tsp. garlic, chopped fine**
 1 **cup white wine**
 2 **cups shellfish stock**
½ **cup cream**
 1 **Tbsp. tomato, chopped fine**
 1 **Tbsp. parsley, chopped fine**
 1 **Tbsp. mushrooms, chopped fine**
 1 **Tbsp. butter**
   Salt and pepper to taste

Sauté the prawns in olive oil for 1 minute or until cooked. Add the shallots and garlic and sauté for 20 seconds. Remove the prawns and reserve. Keep warm.

Deglaze the pan with wine and stock over medium-low heat. Add the cream, tomato, parsley and mushrooms, reducing the sauce by half. Add the butter and salt and pepper to taste.

Drizzle sauce over the prawns before serving.

Prawns Sambucca

Serves 4
Preparation Time: 30 Minutes

¼ cup olive oil
1 Tbsp. garlic, chopped
1 Tbsp. shallots, chopped
16 prawns
¼ cup Chardonnay or dry white wine
¼ cup Sambucca liqueur
¼ cup tomato, diced
1 Tbsp. tarragon, chopped
8 Tbsps. (1 stick) sweet butter
  Salt and pepper to taste
1 lb. angel hair pasta

In a sauté pan, heat the oil over medium-low heat. Add the garlic, shallots and prawns, cooking for 1 to 2 minutes. Add the wine and Sambucca liqueur.

Add the tomatoes, tarragon and butter. Season to taste with salt and pepper. Allow the sauce to reduce and thicken slightly.

Cook the pasta in boiling salted water until al dente.

Serve the prawns and sauce over the pasta.

Swordfish Steak
with Sundried Tomato Tapenade

Serves 4
Preparation Time: 25 Minutes (note marinating time)

- 1 cup sun-dried tomatoes, chopped
- ¼ cup pine nuts, toasted
- 1 Tbsp. garlic, chopped
- 1 Tbsp. parsley, chopped
- 4 Tbsps. capers
- ⅓ cup olive oil
- ⅓ cup balsamic vinegar
- 2 Tbsps. red peppers, roasted, diced
   Salt and pepper to taste
- 4 swordfish steaks

Soften the chopped sun-dried tomatoes in hot water for 1 minute. Place in a mixing bowl with the pine nuts, garlic, parsley, capers, olive oil, vinegar and red peppers. Add salt and pepper to taste. Allow the mixture to marinate in the refrigerator for several hours or overnight.

Grill the swordfish steaks over high heat about 3 to 4 minutes per side. The steaks should be seared on the outside and just cooked through.

Remove steaks from heat and top each steak with 2 Tbsps. tapenade.

Osso Buco

Serves 4
Preparation Time: 45 Minutes
Cooking Time: 3½ Hours
Pre-heat oven to 400°

1 cup unbleached all-purpose flour
Salt and pepper to taste
½ cup olive oil
4 veal shanks, about 4" thick or ½ lb. each
4 onions, peeled, chopped
2 carrots, peeled, chopped
4 celery stalks, chopped
4 tomatoes, diced, seeded
¼ cup basil, chopped
2 tsps. fresh thyme
4 bay leaves
2 cups dry white wine
2 cups orange juice
2 oranges, cut in quarters
2 qts. beef or veal stock

Season the flour with salt and pepper and dredge the pieces of veal shank in it. Shake off any excess.

Heat the oil in a large flameproof casserole or Dutch oven, and quickly sear the veal over medium-high heat, browning it well on all sides. Remove the veal from the pot and add the onions, carrots, celery and tomatoes. Sauté about 4 minutes. Add the herbs and sauté 1 minute. Add the wine, orange juice, oranges and stock. Return the shanks to the pot, season with salt and pepper. Bring mixture to a boil, cover and transfer the pot to the pre-heated oven for approximately 3 hours. A knife inserted into the shank should go in easily.

Remove the oranges and puree the remaining vegetables in small amounts in a food processor. Place the pureed vegetables with the veal shanks over medium heat, bringing the vegetable puree to a boil.

Serve immediately with soft polenta or rice.

Apple Filled Purse with a Cherry & Cassis Creme Anglaise

Serves 4
Preparation Time: 45 Minutes

4 large baking apples,
  Granny Smith
½ cup raisins
¼ cups Cassis
5 Tbsps. butter
3 Tbsps. sugar
½ cup hazelnuts, ground

¼ tsp. cinnamon
1 cup unbleached
  all-purpose flour
¼ tsp. salt
1 cup milk
⅓ cup water
3 eggs

Peel and core the apples and cut into ½" slices.

Soak the raisins in the Cassis

Sauté the apples in 2 Tbsps. butter over medium-low heat. Add 2 Tbsps. sugar and caramelize. Add the hazelnuts, raisins and cinnamon. Set aside.

Prepare the crepe mixture by combining the flour, 1 Tbsp. sugar and salt in a food processor briefly. With the motor running, add the milk, water, eggs and 3 Tbsps. melted butter. Process until smooth.

Heat a heavy 7" nonstick skillet until quite hot. Pour in 3 Tbsps. of the batter, then quickly tilt the pan so the batter spreads evenly, forming a crepe. Cook until lightly brown, 30 to 45 seconds; then turn and cook another 15 seconds. Repeat, using up all the batter.

Place apple mixture in the center of each crepe. Fold up edges to the center. Place in a 300° oven for 15 minutes until warmed. Serve garnished with Sauce Anglaise.

Sauce Anglaise

4 egg yolks
¼ cup sugar

1 cup whipping cream
½ tsp. vanilla

In a mixing bowl, whip the egg yolks and sugar together.

Over medium heat, bring the cream to a boil. Add the egg mixture and cook until the sides bubble. Allow to cool before serving over the apple purses.

TARPY'S ROADHOUSE

AMERICAN CUISINE
Highway 68 & Canyon Del Rey
Monterey
647-1444
Lunch 11:30AM–5PM Monday–Saturday
Dinner 5PM–10PM
Sunday Brunch 10AM–3PM
AVERAGE DINNER FOR TWO: $35

THIS CHARMING, vine-covered stone house brings back the popularity of "Roadhouse" style food, featuring hearty American fare. Once a ranch house, Tarpy's Roadhouse offers country ambiance with outdoor dining in the courtyard or seating in two light and airy dining rooms.

Much of the produce found on the menu gets its start in the garden behind the restaurant. An extensive luncheon menu includes a variety of starters such as Crispy Haystack Onion Rings, Layered Garden Vegetable Terrine and Sourdough Bruschetta with Sonoma Goat Cheese, Roasted Garlic and Sundried Tomatoes. A large selection of fresh salads and sandwiches such as Seared, Peppered Ahi Tuna with Field Greens and Tarpy's Cobb Salad with Gorgonzola Vinaigrette as well as the Oak Grilled Black Angus Cheeseburger are among the tempting favorites.

Dinner specialties from the ranch include Tarpy's Grilled Vegetable Plate with Sweet Corn Succotash, Smoky BBQ Baby Back Ribs with Rosemary Roasted Potatoes and Classic Meatloaf with Mushroom Gravy. Fresh local fish and range-fed poultry round out the menu.

Comfortable as the restaurant is, excellent cuisine is the real reason to come to Tarpy's Roadhouse Restaurant.

Menu for Four

Cajun Spiced Prawns
Rosemary Lamb Loin
Berry Angel Food Cake

Cajun Spiced Prawns

Serves 4
Preparation Time: 30 Minutes

½ tsp. garlic, chopped
1 tsp. shallots, chopped
4 Tbsps. butter
¾ cup beer
¾ cup chicken stock
⅛ tsp. cayenne
¼ tsp. black pepper
1 tsp. kosher salt
½ tsp. fresh rosemary, chopped
½ tsp. fresh thyme, chopped
4 dashes Worcestershire sauce
5 dashes Tabasco sauce
24 prawns, cleaned
1 tsp. lemon juice
4 cups shoestring potatoes, cooked
1 Tbsp. Italian parsley, chopped, plus 4 sprigs for garnish

Sauté the garlic and shallots in 1 Tbsp. butter. Add the beer and stock. Reduce by ⅓. Add the cayenne, black pepper, salt, rosemary, thyme, Worcestershire and Tabasco to the sauce. Add the prawns and poach until just cooked through.

Remove the prawns from the sauce and add the remaining butter to the sauce, reducing while whisking. Remove from heat and finish with the lemon.

On each warmed serving plate, mound the shoestring potatoes in the center and place the prawns leaning against the potatoes. Pour the sauce over the prawns and sprinkle with parsley sprigs.

Rosemary Lamb Loin with Burgundy Wine Syrup

Serves 4
Preparation Time: 45 Minutes (note marinating time)

8 lamb loins, 4 oz. each
2 Tbsps. shallots, minced
1 Tbsp. + 1 tsp. garlic, minced
½ tsp. black pepper, ground
¼ cup olive oil
1 tsp. lemon juice
1 bottle (750ml) Burgundy wine
3 sprigs thyme
3 sprigs parsley
2 Tbsps. honey
2 Tbsps. rice wine vinegar

Prepare the marinade by combining 1 Tbsp. shallots, 1 tsp. minced garlic, black pepper, olive oil and lemon juice. Marinate the lamb for a minimum of four hours to overnight.

Prepare the Burgundy wine syrup by combining the wine, thyme, parsley, honey and rice wine vinegar over low heat. Simmer until reduced to 1 cup liquid. Strain and set aside.

Grill the lamb to your desired temperature.

To serve, slice the lamb on the bias and fan out on plate. Drizzle with the Burgundy Wine Syrup.

Berry Angel Food Cake

Yield: 1 Cake
Pre-heat oven to 325°

10 large egg whites, at room temperature
⅓ tsp. cream of tartar
1 Tbsp. vanilla extract
½ tsp. salt
2¼ cups sugar
1½ cups cake flour
1⅓ pt. raspberries
1 pt. strawberries
1 Tbsp. lemon juice
Mint sprigs, garnish
Powdered sugar, garnish

Whip the egg whites to soft peaks. Gently fold in the cream of tartar, vanilla, salt, 2 cups sugar and the cake flour. Gently fold in ⅓ pt. raspberries.

Spoon the mixture into an ungreased 10-inch nonstick tube pan, and bake at 325° for 50 minutes or until a toothpick inserted in the cake comes out clean.

Invert the pan onto a cake rack and let it cool completely.

Prepare the strawberry sauce by pureeing the strawberries with 4 Tbsps. sugar and the lemon juice to taste. Set aside.

When the cake is cool, invert the pan onto a serving platter. Remove the pan carefully, loosening the cake slightly around the edges with a knife if necessary.

Serve the cake with the strawberry puree and the reserved raspberries. Garnish with mint sprigs and dust with powdered sugar.

WHALING STATION INN RESTAURANT

ITALIAN CUISINE
763 Wave Street
Monterey, CA 93940
373-3778
Dinner nightly 5PM–11PM
AVERAGE DINNER FOR TWO: $45

FAMED FOR ITS uncompromising quality of ingredients and for the originality of chef/owner John Pisto, the Whaling Station Inn is an extraordinary regional restaurant with a national reputation.

One block up from Cannery Row, The Whaling Station is a cozy, upscale haven where hearty conversation, great food and wine and expert service prevail. A secret place that local residents and business executives would prefer to keep to themselves.

The historic exterior of the restaurant hints at the traditional spirit to be found within. As you pass through the vine-covered entry into the large lounge, one senses the relaxing, intimate and elegant ambience.

THE WHALING STATION INN
RESTAURANT

Menu for Four

The Fabulous Artichoke
Spicy Prawns
Pasta with Pancetta and Peas
Grilled Monterey Salmon with Salsa
Long Stemmed Strawberries
with Grand Marnier and White Chocolate

The Fabulous Artichoke

Serves 4
Preparation Time: One Hour

4 large artichokes
¼ cup mayonnaise
¼ cup vinaigrette

Steam artichokes until you can pierce the bottom with a fork, approximately 45 minutes to one hour.

Open the artichoke like a lotus flower. Put a dab of mayonnaise on the heart and pour a vinaigrette over the entire artichoke.

Serve with crusty French bread. Enjoy!

Spicy Prawns

Serves 4
Preparation Time: 1½ Hours

    16 large prawns
     1 Tbsp. ground coriander
     4 chiles (2 chopped fine, 2 cut into strips)
     1 tsp. salt
  1½ cups vegetable oil
     1 tsp. fish sauce
     6 sprigs coriander

Peel and devein the prawns, leaving the shell on the tail only. Rinse prawns with cold water and pat dry with paper towels. Rub the prawns with ground coriander, chopped chiles, salt and a little oil. Let stand for one hour.

Reserve the marinade. Heat the oil in a sauté pan, over medium high heat and sauté the prawns for 2 minutes on each side. Place prawns on a serving plate.

Using the remaining oil, stir into reserved marinade and bring to a quick boil. Add the fish sauce.

Pour over the prawns and garnish with sprigs of coriander and chile strips.

Pasta with Pancetta and Peas

Serves 4
Preparation Time: 45 Minutes

½ **lb. Italian dried pasta**
1 **cup pancetta (Italian bacon) cubed**
½ **cup onion, chopped**
3 **garlic cloves, chopped**
4 **cups tomatoes, chopped**
1 **cup baby peas**
 Salt and pepper to taste
½ **cup Romano cheese, grated**

Cook the pasta al dente.

Sauté the pancetta, onions and garlic until brown. Add the tomatoes and peas. Season with salt and pepper.

Pour the sauce over the hot pasta. Sprinkle freshly-ground Romano cheese over the sauce and serve.

Grilled Salmon with Salsa

Serves 4
Preparation Time: 45 Minutes

Four 8 oz. salmon steaks
¼ cup olive oil
2 tomatoes, chopped
1 clove garlic
¼ cup cilantro, chopped
Juice of 2 limes
Tabasco to taste
Salt and pepper

Rub the salmon with olive oil, salt and pepper. Grill over a low flame, cooking slowly. Turn only once and remove when fish is opaque.

To make salsa, combine tomatoes, garlic and cilantro. Add the lime juice and season with Tabasco and salt and pepper to taste.

Long-Stemmed Strawberries with Grand Marnier and White Chocolate

Serves 4
Preparation Time: 25 minutes (note refrigeration time)

16 long-stemmed strawberries
32 oz. white chocolate
** 8 oz. Grand Marnier**
Empty egg carton
Hypodermic needle

Rinse and clean the strawberries well.
Melt the white chocolate in a double boiler on medium heat. Dip half of the strawberry in the white chocolate.

Quickly remove the strawberry and insert, with the white chocolate side up, into an empty egg carton to cool. Continue until all the strawberries are dipped.

Refrigerate for at least 1½ hours.
Before serving, inject each strawberry with ½ oz. Grand Marnier.

PACIFIC GROVE:
NO LONGER BLUE

PACIFIC GROVE'S restrictive roots as a religious retreat were so pervasive that you couldn't buy a drink there until 1969. The liquor ban had been in effect for 96 years.

The grandeur of the Pacific Grove coast has always drawn visitors. Inland Indian tribes used to vacation there while seeking mussels, abalone, fish and tule elk. And, as early as the 17th century, Point Pinos was used as a landmark by Manila galleons on their way to Mexico.

But Pacific Grove (the locals call it P.G.) got its start in 1875, with the establishment of a Methodist summer retreat. The Methodists stayed in tents and, before long, began building Victorian homes right over their tents.

In contrast to the wild and woolly origins of other communities in the area, the pioneers of P.G. established a long list of restrictive blue laws. For instance, one blue law specified in detail the type of bathing suits that could be worn and other laws banned swimming, boating or fishing on Sundays. Only medicine could be sold on Sundays. Deeds to property banned all kinds of gambling, billiards, dancing, swearing and boisterous talk. Liquor could not be sold, bought or even given away.

A CURFEW BANNED anyone under age 18 from the streets after 8 p.m. in the winter and 9 p.m. in the summer. One law stipulated that all window shades had to be kept up until 10 p.m., so constables could peek in the windows, on the lookout for illicit hanky-panky.

Graceful glass-bottomed boats at Pacific Grove's Lovers Point.

ONE 1879 visitor, novelist Robert Louis Stevenson, had this to say about the Methodist retreat: "Thither, in the warm season, crowds came to enjoy a life of teetotalism, religion, and flirtation, which I am willing to think blameless and agreeable."

The final straw among the restrictions was the fence with locked gate that encircled the retreat. Designed to keep out undesirables, including peddlers from sinful Monterey, the locked gate and rigmarole required to get in and out led to a revolt.

In 1880, State Senator Benjamin Langford, tired of having to hike a mile to the retreat office to get the key to unlock the gate, took an axe to the gate. The gate was never replaced and nine years later, in 1889, the city was incorporated.

By 1880, lots in P.G. cost from $135 to $250. Furnished three-bedroom homes could be bought for $650.

A LOT OF THINGS have changed in Pacific Grove. But what hasn't changed is the spectacular location overlooking Monterey Bay and the Pacific Ocean, particularly when one travels on the five miles of scenic road that hugs the remarkable coast.

Take Ocean View Blvd. (try it on a bike) starting at the aquarium. Include a picnic lunch. You may see playful sea otters breaking shellfish on rocks they carry on their chests, sea lions perched atop rocks and looking like futuristic sculptures or squadrons of brown pelicans swooping low over the water in search of lunch.

THIS STRETCH of coast is one of the best places in the world to spot the massive grey whales that pass by on their annual migration from Alaska to Baja California, where they breed. The whales take a short break in their migration to take in the sights of Monterey Bay. The migration begins in November, but the best time to see them spouting and leaping is January. One of the best spots to see them from shore is Lovers Point.

Along the shore, you will pass spectacular bed and breakfast inns with inspiring views of the ever-changing bay, a pathway afire with the "magic carpet" of bright pink ice plant blossoms, and massive tide pools teeming with plant and animal life.

Fishing boats often congregate off the P.G. shore, even at night, when the squid boats work with bright lights upon the water.

LOVERS POINT, a favorite spot for outdoor weddings, is a great place to spread out a picnic blanket on the lawn or the beach and watch the surfers. The sheltered beach was blasted out with dynamite in 1904 by William Smith. With the rock he blasted loose, Smith also built the stone wall and pier that still stand. In the old days, glass-bottomed boats explored the kelp forest and its wealth of sea life. Today, scuba divers flock to the point's underwater wonderland.

Lovers Point is the site of the major events of the Feast of Lanterns, celebrated every July. Begun in 1905, the charming pageant recreates the much-altered legend of a wealthy Chinese mandarin who had a beautiful daughter, whom he called Queen Topaz. Promised in marriage to another wealthy mandarin, Topaz instead fell in love with a poor student and ran away with him. In the original story, based on the Blue Willow china pattern, the lovesick girl drowned herself rather than marry a man she didn't love. In the P.G. version, Topaz and the poor student depart in a burst of fireworks, as Monarch butterflies. But not to worry: they return for the pageant every year.

The Pacific Ocean and Monterey Bay converge at Point Pinos, the northern tip of the Monterey Peninsula. You may want to visit the lighthouse, built in 1855. But be careful on the road—the foghorn may startle you if it goes off.

FURTHER DOWN Sunset Drive, past the Great Tide Pool and the rolling sand dunes and partially hidden among the pine trees, stands the Asilomar Conference grounds. Early plans for the grounds and the structures were developed by Julia Morgan, architect of the Hearst Castle at San Simeon.

Architecture plays a large role in P.G. Many of the old homes have been preserved and restored. In wandering through town, you may notice small signs on some of the older homes. The signs indicate when the houses were built and the name of the original owner. Some of the mansions and larger homes have been converted into bed and breakfast inns. The Victorian Home Tour, part of the P.G. Good Old Days celebration in April, is a good opportunity to get inside a selection of the best buildings.

Another event worthy of note in P.G. is the annual Butterfly Parade, held every October. The parade gives the town's schoolchildren a chance to march through town in a colorful variety of costumes, mostly of Monarch butterflies.

GREAT FLOCKS of the orange and black butterflies arrive each year in October and November and spend the winter in P.G. Sometimes there are so many that they cover the branches and leaves of the "butterfly trees."

Visitors should note St. Mary's by-the-Sea Episcopal Church, the oldest church in town. Built in 1887, the beautiful wooden church boasts two exquisite Tiffany stained-glass windows.

Also worth a visit are the P.G. Museum of Natural History and nearby historic Chautauqua Hall, where Pacific Grove was born amid Methodist meetings and lectures.

PACIFIC GROVE DATEBOOK: Wildflower Show at P.G. Museum, April; P.G. Good Old Days, Quilt Show and Victorian Home Tour, also in April; Feast of Lanterns, July; Lovers Point Catamaran Race, September; Butterfly Parade, October; Christmas at the Inns, December.

GOSBY HOUSE INN

643 Lighthouse Avenue
Pacific Grove, CA 93950
375-1287
Rooms $85–$130

WHEN YOU ENTER the Gosby House Inn, you will be greeted by a most warm and hospitable staff. Fine appointments enrich the interior of this magnificently restored Victorian mansion that boasts a collection of rare antiques. An open-hearth fireplace entices visitors to gather and enjoy afternoon tea, sherry, fresh fruits and hors d'oeuvres. Each morning, a delicious breakfast is tastefully prepared and served in the parlor or the garden patio.

The guest rooms were inspired by the romance and luxury of fine European country inns; each room reflects this mood with polished, natural woods, soft comforters, delicately colored wallpapers and flowers. Fireplaces are available in some rooms, and most rooms have a private bath.

The Gosby House Inn is located in the heart of the historic seaside town of Pacific Grove, with its many Victorian homes and beautiful shoreline. It is a truly romantic retreat in a town that time forgot.

Sour Cream Coffeecake

Preparation Time: 1½ Hours
Pre-heat oven to 350°
Yield: 1 bundt pan—10"

1 cup butter (2 sticks) softened
2¾ cups sugar
2 eggs, beaten
⅛ tsp. salt
2 cups sour cream
2 cups white flour
1 Tbsp. baking powder
1 Tbsp. vanilla
2 cups pecans, chopped
2 Tbsps. cinnamon

Grease and flour bundt pan. Cream the butter and 2 cups of the sugar. Add eggs, blend, add the sour cream and vanilla.

Sift together the flour, baking powder and salt. Fold the dry ingredients into the creamed mixture, and beat until just blended. Do not overbeat.

Mix together remaining ¼ cup sugar with pecans and cinnamon.

Pour half of the batter into the bundt pan. Sprinkle with half the pecan and sugar mixture. Add the remaining batter and top with the remaining pecan mixture.

Serve warm.

Lemon Curd

Preparation Time: 15 Minutes

2 cups sugar
12 egg yolks, strained
1 cup lemon juice
1 cup unsalted butter
2 Tbsps. zest of lemon

Combine the sugar and egg yolks in a saucepan. Stir in the lemon juice gradually. Cook over low heat, stirring constantly until mixture coats the back of a spoon. Do not boil. Remove from heat, whisk until cooled. Stir in butter and zest. Cool. Store in refrigerator. Keeps for weeks.

Chocolate Decadence

Serves 10
Preparation Time: 25 Minutes (note refrigeration time)
Pre-heat oven to 425°

1 lb. semisweet chocolate
5 Tbsps. butter
5 large eggs
1 Tbsp. flour
   Whipping cream for garnish

Grease a 9" or 10" cake pan or soufflé dish and line it with wax paper.

Melt the chocolate and butter in a saucepan.

Beat the eggs and flour in a separate bowl and set in a pan of hot water. Blend the chocolate mixture into the egg and flour mixture.

Pour into the cake pan or soufflé dish, and bake 15 minutes at 425°. Cover with foil and freeze after baking.

Garnish with whipped cream.

Steamed Chocolate Almond Pudding

Serves 8
Preparation Time: 1½ Hours

5 oz. semisweet chocolate
3 oz. unsweetened chocolate
½ cup plus 2 Tbsps. butter, softened
⅔ cup sugar
6 egg yolks
⅔ cup finely ground toasted almonds
¼ tsp. almond extract
8 egg whites
Pinch of salt
Whipped cream garnish

Place both chocolates in a bowl. Set over barely simmering water. Stir until melted and smooth. Remove from the heat and cool.

In a mixing bowl, beat the butter and sugar until it is pale yellow and fluffy. Add the yolks and beat until very light, about two minutes. Fold in the almonds, extract and chocolate.

In a large bowl beat the egg whites and a pinch of salt until stiff peaks are formed when the beater is lifted. Fold into the chocolate mixture gently.

Place nuts on the bottom of a fluted pudding mold (8 cup). Spoon the batter into the mold, covering tightly. Add boiling water 1" up the side of the pudding mold.

Simmer gently 50-60 minutes or until a skewer inserted in the center comes out clean. Let cool 5 minutes before unmolding. Serve with whipped cream.

Green Gables Inn

104 Fifth Street
Pacific Grove, CA 93950
(408)375-2095
1-800-841-5252
Rooms $95–$155

THIS ROMANTIC QUEEN Anne-styled mansion by-the-sea will capture your heart and imagination at first sight. A half-timbered, step-gabled residence, built in 1888, the Green Gables is an exquisite gem among Pacific Grove's many Victorian homes. Set on the edge of the Pacific shoreline, the Green Gables enjoys a spectacular panoramic view of Monterey Bay. The fairy-tale setting is further enhanced by the warm personal attention given to the guests.

The parlor features large bay window alcoves facing the bay, a lovely collection of antique furnishings and a unique fireplace framed by stained-glass panels.

In the afternoon, tea, sherry and wine are available in front of a cheery fire. In the morning, a delicious breakfast is served in the dining room with a panoramic view of the bay.

Herbed Roulade

Serves 8
Preparation Time: One Hour
Pre-heat oven to 350°

2 Tbsps. oil
2 eggs
1 cup milk
½ cup flour
2 tsps. fresh chives
1 Tbsp. fresh parsley, chopped
2 tsps. fresh dill

Brush a 11″ × 17″ jelly roll pan with oil.

Beat the eggs for 15 seconds until pale yellow. With a mixer on, add the milk in a slow stream. Add the flour and mix until smooth. Add the herbs. Let the mixture rest for 30 minutes.

Bake for 12 minutes at 350°. Cool in the pan and loosen the bottom with a metal spatula.

Filling

5-6 ripe avocados, chopped
2 onions, chopped
Butter for sautéing
2 cups mushrooms, sliced
1 cup grated cheddar

Sauté onions and mushrooms. Mix all ingredients together. Spread filling over the entire crepe and roll lengthwise.

Heat slightly when ready to slice.

Dutch Baby with Blueberry Compote

Serves 4
Preparation Time: 45 Minutes
Pre-heat oven to 375°

      1 Tbsp. butter
      5 eggs
    ½ cup all-purpose flour
    ¼ cup wheat flour
      Pinch of nutmeg
 2½ cups milk
    ⅓ cup honey
      2 cups blueberries
      Sugar to taste
      3 Tbsps. cornstarch
    ¼ cup cold water

In the oven, melt the butter in a quiche pan, lightly oiling the bottom and sides of pan. Remove from oven and set aside.

In a large mixing bowl, beat the eggs together. Add both the white and wheat flour, nutmeg and milk. Gently fold in the honey until well blended. Pour into the oiled quiche pan and bake for 35-40 minutes.

Prepare the compote in a saucepan by combining the blueberries and sugar. Bring to a soft boil. Slowly mix in the cornstarch with water to a desired consistency.

Serve the hot compote over the Dutch babies.

Tropical Banana Bread

Preparation Time: 1½ hours (note elapsed time)
Pre-heat oven to 350°
Yields: One large loaf

 1 cup currants
½ cup dark rum
 3 cups flour
 1 tsp. salt
 1 tsp. baking soda
 1 tsp. baking powder
 2 tsps. cinnamon
½ tsp. nutmeg
½ cup coconut plus 2 Tbsps. (for topping)
½ cup shortening
 1 cup brown sugar
 2 eggs
⅓ cup buttermilk
 1 cup mashed ripe bananas

In a small bowl steep the currants in heated rum for one hour.

Combine the dry ingredients. Mix the liquid ingredients. Stir together until just combined. Add the rum-soaked currants and pour into a loaf pan.

Sprinkle the top with 2 Tbsps. coconut and bake at 350° for one hour.

THE MARTINE INN

255 Oceanview Blvd.
Pacific Grove, CA 93950
(408)373-3388
Rooms $115–$225

TAKE A STEP BACK in time to gracious living with a complimentary breakfast served on Victorian china, Sheffield silver, crystal and lace.

This grand old home, built in the late 1890s, overlooks the magnificent rocky coastline of Pacific Grove.

Each of the 19 rooms has a private bath and is elegantly furnished with antiques. Many rooms have ocean views and wood-burning fireplaces.

Read in the library, sun-bathe in the landscaped enclosed courtyard, watch whales, sea otters, sailboat races or the fishing fleet from the two sitting rooms. Enjoy yourselves.

Crab and Spinach Crepes

Makes 24 crepes
Preparation Time: 20 Minutes

Crepes

¾ cup flour
2 tsps. sugar
1 tsp. salt
4 eggs
4 egg yolks
1 qt. milk
1 Tbsp. butter

Sift dry ingredients. Beat eggs and milk until blended. Mix the egg mixture into the dry, blend until smooth.

Using clarified butter, cook over a medium heat, 2 Tbsps. of batter per crepe, depending on the thickness desired for the crepes.

Crab and Spinach Filling

1½ cups shredded crab
2 bunches spinach, chopped
Juice of one lemon
1 tsp. dried thyme
1 tsp. dried dill
1½ cups cream cheese
Pepper to taste

Mix all ingredients thoroughly and place 2 Tbsps. of the crab mixture in each crepe.

Salmon Mousse Wellington

Serves 4
Preparation Time: 15 Minutes (note elapsed time)

1 cup flaked salmon
2 green onions chopped
   Juice of one lemon
½ cup mayonnaise
   Dash of hot sauce
1 package gelatin mix
2 cups water—1 cold, 1 hot
1 cup whipped cream
1 sheet frozen puff pastry
   Egg wash

Mix the salmon, green onion, lemon, mayonnaise and hot sauce. In separate bowl combine the gelatin mix with one cup cold water until blended. Mix in hot water and blend all ingredients together. Gently fold in the whipped cream. Refrigerate 4 hours or until set.

Cut the puff pastry into four equal pieces. Fill each pastry piece with ¼ to ½ cup salmon mousse filling. Fold long edges together and press with a fork to seal. Baste with egg wash.

The Salmon Wellington can be served with a hollandaise sauce.

Oriental Chicken Salad

Serves 8
Preparation Time: 25 Minutes (note marinating time)

   5 lbs. chicken breast, cooked and cubed
   1 cup raisins
   2 cups celery, diced
   1 cup walnuts, chopped
   ½ cup pimentos, diced
   2 cups water chestnuts, sliced

Dressing

   2 cups peanut oil
   3 Tbsps. sesame oil
   1½ cups rice wine vinegar
   1½ cups water
   2 Tbsps. honey
   2 Tbsps. soy sauce
   1 Tbsp. lemon juice
   3 garlic cloves, chopped
   ½ tsp. salt
   2 tsps. black pepper
   3 Tbsps. ground ginger
   1 Tbsp. curry
   2 Tbsps. toasted sesame seeds.

   Mix all ingredients for dressing.
   Add chicken, raisins, celery, walnuts, pimentos and water chestnuts.
   Marinate.

Peanut Butter Vegetable Soup

Serves 6
Preparation Time: 25 Minutes

½ cup onion, chopped
1 large carrot, peeled and sliced
1 large stalk celery, chopped
2 garlic cloves, minced or pressed
1 Tbsp. salad oil
1 cup chunk-style peanut butter
8 cups chicken broth
1 medium potato, scrubbed and diced
⅛ tsp. cayenne
3 Tbsps. red wine vinegar
   Salt and pepper to taste
   Chopped peanuts
   Garnish with parsley sprigs

In a 4 qt. pan over medium heat, combine onion, carrot, celery and garlic with oil, stirring often, until onion is limp. Remove from heat and add peanut butter. Stir to blend with the vegetables. Stir in broth, adding potatoes and cayenne. Bring to a boil.

Reduce heat to simmer, cover and cook until potatoes are done, approximately 15 minutes. Add vinegar and salt and pepper to taste.

Garnish with peanuts and parsley.

Lemon Cream Cheese Dessert

Serves 8
Preparation Time: 15 Minutes

1 cup milk
½ cup lemon juice
1 lb. soft cream cheese
1 cup sugar
2 packages lemon Jello
3 cups water

Blend the milk, lemon juice, cream cheese and sugar together. Gently fold in two packages of lemon Jello and water. Spoon into 8 sherbet cups or champagne glasses.

Let mixture set before adding Sour Lemon Topping.

Sour Lemon Topping

½ cup lemon juice
½ cup water
½ cup sugar
4 eggs

Blend together all ingredients. Over medium heat bring to a boil stirring constantly. When mixture has thickened, remove from heat and cool before spreading the topping.

PACIFIC GROVE INN

581 Pine Ave.
Pacific Grove, CA 93950
(408)375-2825
Rooms $70.50–$90.50

THE INN HAS 10 suites, decorated with the Queen Anne-style cherry furniture, matching fabrics and wallpapers and brass beds. Each guestroom has a gas fireplace, full bath and a small refrigerator. Some of the guest rooms have bay views.

The Pacific Grove Inn opened in May, 1986 after a year-long restoration of this magnificent Victorian, built in 1904. The house is now listed in the National Register of Historic Places.

Crab and Three Cheese Strata

Serves 12
Preparation Time: 45 Minutes (note elapsed time)
Pre-heat oven to 350°

```
 1 loaf sourdough bread, cubed
 1 cup ricotta cheese
½ lb. Dungeness crab meat
¼ lb. shredded Monterey Jack cheese
¼ lb. shredded sharp cheddar cheese
 2 Tbsps. chopped green chiles
12 eggs, slightly beaten
 6 cups milk
 5 Tbsps. melted butter
¼ tsp. dry mustard
```

Butter a 9″ × 14″ baking dish. Layer the bread with ricotta, crab, Jack and cheddar cheese and chiles.

Blend eggs, milk, butter and mustard in a large pouring bowl. Pour over bread mixture, covering all of it.

Cover the Strata with plastic wrap and refrigerate overnight.

Bake at 350° for 30 minutes or until eggs are set.

SEVEN GABLES INN

555 Ocean View Blvd.
Pacific Grove, CA 93950
(408)372-4341
Rooms $95–$165

THE SEVEN GABLES Inn is a century-old Victorian mansion situated on the very edge of Monterey Bay. All guest rooms have panoramic ocean views and private baths. A very generous light breakfast is served in the formal dining room each morning. Four o'clock high tea is set out on the inviting sunporch featuring an unparallelled view of the bay and rocky coastline.

The furnishings throughout the Inn are formal Victorian and feature fine European, Oriental and American antiques. Intricate Persian carpets, crystal chandeliers, inlaid sideboards, beveled-glass armoires and gilt pier mirrors set an elegant atmosphere.

Owner-operated by the Flatley family, the Inn's atmosphere is one of careful attention to detail, friendliness and quiet hospitality reminiscent of an earlier time.

Apple Harvest Muffins

Preparation Time: 45 Minutes
Pre-heat oven to 325°
Yields 1½ dozen large muffins

2¾ cups flour
 ¾ cup unprocessed bran
  1 cup sugar
  1 cup brown sugar (packed)
1½ Tbsps. cinnamon
  3 tsps. baking powder
1½ tsps. salt
  1 tsp. baking soda
1¼ cups oil
1½ tsps. vanilla
  4 eggs
  3 ripe apples, peeled, cored and chopped

In a large bowl combine flour, bran, sugars, cinnamon, baking powder, salt and baking soda and mix very thoroughly. Add oil, vanilla, eggs and chopped apples. Mix just until blended.

Fill greased muffin tins ¾ full. Bake at 325° for 25-30 minutes or until brown.

Cool, remove from pan and serve warm with butter, favorite preserves or just plain.

CENTRAL 159 CATERING

CALIFORNIA CUISINE
529 Central Avenue
Pacific Grove
655-4280

THIS SMALL MASTERPIECE of a restaurant opened in Pacific Grove in 1987, developing a list of loyal and enthusiastic regulars. Today, Central 159 specializes in catering private parties with customized menus.

Chef/owner David Beckwith has a continuing tradition of using fresh produce and meats of the highest quality. It's a custom that pays off in exceptionally fine flavors and textures.

Menu for Six

Grilled Zesty Prawns
Smoked Trout Chowder
Wilted Spinach Salad
Taipei Grilled Chicken Breasts
Flourless Chocolate Pecan Cake

Grilled Zesty Prawns

Serves 6
Preparation Time: 10 Minutes (note marinating time)

 4 cloves garlic, peeled, chopped
 1 roasted serrano chile pepper, peeled, seeded
 1 bunch cilantro, chopped
   Juice of 3 lemons
 1 bunch scallions, diced
 1 Anahiem or ancho chile pod
 2 cups peanut or olive oil (to cover only)
24 jumbo prawns

In a large mixing bowl, combine the garlic, serrano pepper, cilantro, lemon juice and scallions.

Cut or tear the ancho chile into the marinade mixture and toss. Add half the volume of oil and pour over prawns. Add remaining oil only if necessary to evenly coat the prawns. Marinate for 2 hours.

Grill for 2 minutes on each side.

Cooking tip: Do not float the prawns in the marinade; that will dilute the flavors.

Smoked Trout Chowder

Serves 6
Preparation Time: 45 Minutes

   2 Tbsps. butter
   ¼ cup peanut oil
   3 cloves garlic, finely chopped
   2 carrots, peeled, chopped
   1 medium red onion, diced
   1 large red bell pepper, diced
   1 large green bell pepper, diced
   2 medium leeks, diced
   1 small jalapeño pepper, skinned, seeded
1½ cups white wine
1½ cups fish or chicken stock
   1 lb. smoked trout, coarsely chopped
   6 small red potatoes, cooked
   3 Tbsps. fresh thyme
   2 cups milk
   2 cups half and half

In a 4 quart pot, melt butter in the peanut oil over high heat. Add the garlic, carrots, onion, peppers, leeks and jalapeño. Cook until tender.

Add white wine and cook 5 minutes.

Add stock, trout and potatoes. Let simmer 10 minutes.

Add thyme, milk and half and half and cook for 30 minutes.

Pour into oversized bowls and serve with a garlic crouton, fresh chopped Italian parsley or with a float of roasted garlic.

Cooking tip: This chowder makes a great entree by itself with a loaf of crusty sourdough bread.

Wilted Spinach Salad

Serves 6
Preparation Time: 10 Minutes

 12 cloves garlic, peeled
1½ Tbsps. Dijon mustard
  1 cup sherry vinegar
  3 cups olive or peanut oil
  2 bunches fresh spinach, cleaned, stemmed

Place garlic, mustard and vinegar in food processor or blender and process until garlic is completely chopped. With the processor running, slowly drizzle in oil continuously until dressing is completely emulsified.

Serve dressing either hot or cold using ¼ cup of dressing per serving.

Coat spinach leaves completely before serving.

Taipei Grilled Chicken Breasts

Serves 6
Preparation Time: 20 Minutes (note marinating time)

    1 cup Hoisin sauce
    ¼ cup red wine vinegar
    2 Tbsps. black bean paste
    4 cloves garlic, diced
    1 Two-inch piece fresh ginger, peeled, grated
    4 scallions, chopped
    1 Tbsp. soy sauce
    1 Tbsp. dry mustard
    1 Tbsp. Tabasco
    ¼ cup peanut oil
    6 chicken breasts

Combine all ingredients in a medium mixing bowl except for the peanut oil and chicken.

Briskly whip in the peanut oil and baste over chicken breasts. Marinate for 2 hours prior to grilling or baking chicken.

Allow 15 minutes if chicken is to be grilled and 30 minutes to cook chicken in the oven.

Cooking tip: This sauce is an excellent dipping sauce on the side for chicken, pork, veal or rabbit and will store up to 2 weeks in the refrigerator.

Flourless Chocolate Pecan Cake

Yield: 2 10-inch cakes
Preparation Time: One hour
Pre-heat oven to 425°

½ lb. unsalted butter
¾ lb. semisweet chocolate
2 Tbsps. brandy
12 eggs, separated
1½ cups sugar
3 cups pecans, chopped

Combine butter, chocolate and brandy and melt in a double boiler or in a bowl over a pot of boiling water. Remove from heat.

In a large bowl, beat egg yolks and 1 cup sugar together until light and fluffy. Fold in the melted chocolate and chopped pecans.

In a separate bowl, beat egg whites to a soft peak, slowly adding the remaining ½ cup of sugar. Fold beaten egg whites into the batter. Do not over-stir.

Divide batter evenly between two 10-inch greased spring form pans.

Bake for 40 minutes or until a knife inserted in the center comes out clean.

Cooking tip: Serve with chocolate sauce, fresh berries and/or whipped cream.

EL COCODRILO

CARIBBEAN/SOUTH AMERICAN CUISINE
701 Lighthouse Ave.
Pacific Grove
655-3311
Appetizers, beer and wine bar 4PM
Dinner 5PM–10PM
Closed Tuesday
AVERAGE DINNER FOR TWO: $25

EL COCODRILO ("the crocodile" in Spanish) captures the spirit and flavor of tropical America. The menu features fresh seafood and produce available from the seas and fields around the Monterey Peninsula, with recipes from the Caribbean, Central and South America.

The ravishing tapestry of flavors, textures and colors is indicative of chef owner Julio Ramirez's cooking. El Cocodrilo is a place where you can take people who don't normally like ethnic food. The menu here is always lovely, light and clean. There are hand-made Nicaraguan tamales, Jamaican curry crab cakes, Amazon catfish, West Indian smoked ribs, Mayan chicken, Bahamian seafood chowder and an assortment of fresh salads and house-made desserts. A fine selection of California wines is offered by the bottle or by the glass. The beer selection includes varieties from Brazil and Africa.

Framed photographs by proprietor Marie Perucca-Ramirez showcase her travels in Central and South America. The walls are gaily decorated with feather necklaces and masks from the Amazon, as well as pottery and air plants from the Central American rain forest. The restaurant donates a percentage of sales to the Orinoco Crocodile Project in Venezuela.

El Cocodrilo

ROTISSERIE and SEAFOOD GRILL

Menu for Four

Sweet Corn Tamales
Seafood Caldo
Chicken Breast Criollo

Sweet Corn Tamales

Serves 8
Preparation Time: 1½ Hours

6 ears of fresh corn
½ cup corn meal
½ cup masa harina (finely ground corn meal)
1 tsp. salt
½ cup margarine
   Black beans, optional
   Crème fraîche, optional

Remove the corn husks and save for the tamales. With a knife, shave the corn kernels from the husks. Place the kernels in a blender and purée. Place the corn purée in a mixing bowl and add the corn meal and masa harina. Add the salt and margarine and mix thoroughly.

Take the corn husks, put enough dough in each to make a finger sized tamal, then fold the husk around the filling, making a neat, secure "envelope."

Steam the tamales in standing position for 1¼ hours.

Serve with black beans and crème fraiche.

Cooking tip: The corn meal and the masa harina are to tighten up the mixture and give proper consistency to the dough. Add more or less depending on the moistness of the corn purée.

Seafood Caldo

Serves 4
Preparation Time: 15 Minutes

1 cup scallops
1 cup rock shrimp
2 filets snapper or rock cod, 8 oz. each, cut in cubes
8 mussels in their shells, cleaned
4 cups water
1 cup tomatoes, diced
¼ cup red onion, diced
¼ cup jicama, diced
¼ cup carrots, julienne
1 serrano chile, minced fine
2 Tbsps. cilantro, chopped
Juice of 1 lime
Salt and pepper to taste

Rinse the seafood in cold water, drain and place in a pot. Add the water. Over medium heat, bring the pot to simmer. Continue to simmer until the mussels open, then add the tomatoes, onion, jicama, carrots and chile. Bring the pot to a simmer again, then finish the soup by adding the cilantro and lime juice. Season with salt and pepper to taste.

Serve immediately—the vegetables should be crisp and fresh, not overcooked.

Chicken Breast Criollo

Serves 4
Preparation Time: 15 Minutes (note marinating time)

4 chicken breasts, boneless
½ cup soy sauce
½ cup peanut oil
1 tsp. Cajun spices
1 tsp. black pepper
1 Tbsp. achiote paste
1 tsp. garlic, puréed

Pound the chicken breasts to ¼-inch thick. Set aside.

Prepare the marinade by mixing the soy sauce, peanut oil, Cajun spices, pepper, achiote paste and garlic. Allow the chicken to marinate for 2 hours before cooking.

Grill the breasts or sauté them for 3 minutes on each side.

Cooking tip: Achiote is a spice blend of ground annatto seeds, cumin, vinegar, garlic and other spices. Achiote paste is available in the gourmet section of many food and specialty stores.

FANDANGO RESTAURANT

COUNTRY MEDITERRANEAN
223 17th Street
Pacific Grove
373-0588
Lunch daily 11AM–2PM
Dinner nightly 5:30PM–10PM
Sunday brunch 10AM–2:30PM
AVERAGE DINNER FOR TWO: $45

FANDANGO BRINGS TOGETHER the flavors of the world's prized culinary regions. North African couscous…Spanish paella and tapas…Canneloni Niçoise…these are examples of the world of wonderful food the Fandango chef, Pedro De La Cruz, produces every day.

Whether your mood is carefree or quiet, social or private, Fandango has a dining area to suit you. Spend an intimate evening in the dining room, accented with fresh flowers and fireside dining. Celebrate a special occasion in the stonewalled wine cellar, privately tucked down stairs. Enjoy the perfumed aromas from the wood grill in the terrace room or soak up the sun on the outdoor patio. Enjoy!

fandango

Menu for Six

Salade Niçoise
Paella
Creme Brulée

Salade Niçoise

Serves 6
Preparation Time: 25 Minutes

1 head butter lettuce or red lettuce
2 medium tomatoes, quartered
⅓ green, red and yellow bell pepper, cut in ¼ inch strips
1 heart of celery, diced
½ cucumber, peeled and sliced
3 green onions, chopped
1 medium potato, boiled and diced in ½" cubes
1 cup cooked green string beans
1 cup canned tuna, drained (preferably water-packed)
6-12 anchovy filets
½ cup Nicoise olives (packed in brine, not oil)
3 hard-boiled eggs, quartered
 Several fresh basil leaves, chopped
 Vinaigrette

Arrange lettuce around a salad bowl. Place tomato quarters on tops of lettuce leaves. Combine bell peppers, celery, cucumber, potatoes and green beans and arrange decoratively on top of tomatoes. Sprinkle the tuna and chopped basil on top of vegetables. Top each salad with 1 or 2 anchovy filets, 2 egg quarters, a few olives and green onions.

Dress the salad with vinaigrette immediately before serving and toss lightly.

Paella

Serves 6
Preparation Time: 1½ Hours

Olive oil
2 medium onions, chopped
2 cloves garlic, chopped
1 chorizo sausage (about ½
  lb.) sliced ½ inch thick
1 large tomato, diced
3 Tbsps. parsley, chopped
2 large pinches of saffron
  threads
3 cups chicken broth
1½ cups white rice (do not
  use quick-cooking rice)

4 lbs. chicken, boned
½ lb. scallops
½ lb. calamari, sliced in
  1-inch pieces
½ lb. shrimp, peeled with
  tails intact
6 littleneck clams
6 mussels
1 cup frozen peas
Fresh parsley for garnish

Set aside 1½ cups of chicken broth and soak saffron in remaining broth.

In a paella pan, very large skillet or wok, heat olive oil and cook onions and garlic until they are transparent. Add chorizo, parsley and all but 2 Tbsps. of the tomato and cook until chorizo is browned. Add chicken and cook 5-10 minutes or until chicken is firm. Stir in rice and reserved chicken broth, cover and cook over low heat for 20 minutes.

After 20 minutes, stir in calamari and remaining broth with saffron, cover again and cook another 20 minutes.

Now stir in scallops and shrimp, cover and cook 10 minutes.

Stir in mussels, clams, reserved tomato and frozen peas and cook just until shellfish open.

Garnish with fresh parsley and serve at once, in the pan.

Creme Brulée

Serves 6
Preparation Time: 20 Minutes (note elapsed time)

   2 cups heavy cream
   1-inch piece of vanilla bean
   12 egg yolks
   ½ cup sugar
   ¼ cup powdered sugar

Combine cream and vanilla bean in a medium saucepan and scald. Do not boil. Remove from heat.

In a separate bowl, beat egg yolks and slowly blend in the ½ cup of sugar. Adding slowly, pour the scalded cream into the egg and sugar mixture. Place combined ingredients in the top of a double boiler and stir over medium heat until the custard thickens on the back of a wooden spoon.

Pour into 6 custard ramekins and cool to room temperature. Refrigerate until serving time.

When you are ready to serve, sprinkle the powdered sugar over the custards, making sure to cover the entire surface evenly. Glaze under broiler, or if available, with a hot round brulée iron, until the sugar turns medium to medium dark brown. Serve immediately.

THE FISHWIFE RESTAURANT

SEAFOOD SPECIALTIES
1996 Sunset Drive
Pacific Grove
375-7107
Lunch and dinner Wednesday–Monday 11 AM–10PM
Closed Tuesday
AVERAGE DINNER FOR TWO: $20

WHERE TO GO for well-prepared fresh fish? The Fishwife, of course, which is deservedly famous for its excellent variety of seafood and pasta dishes. Travels of chef/owner Julio Ramirez through Central and South America as well as the Caribbean have enriched his innovative menu.

Recipes for sauces and salsas are influenced by the availability of seasonal fruits and vegetables as well as fresh herbs and spices. Daily specials from the grill reflect the catch of the day from local waters. House specialties include calamari, swordfish, halibut, mussels, prawns, catfish, sole and tilapia in unique presentations. The salads are innovative and the desserts are made fresh on the premises daily.

The Fishwife has won numerous awards. Both the Pacific Grove and Seaside restaurants have consistently been voted "Best Seafood in Monterey County."

The Pacific Grove Fishwife theme colors are appropriate oceanic shades of blue. Large windows look out onto the nearby dunes and sea.

Menu for Four

New Zealand Mussels in Cilantro &
Serrano Cream Sauce with Salsa Fresca
Boston Clam Chowder
Mixed Greens with Roasted Pecans and
Honey Mustard Vinaigrette
Tilapia Cancun with Green Cashew Sauce
Caribbean Cole Slaw
Key Lime Pie

Salsa Fresca

Preparation Time: 10 Minutes

½ jicama, peeled, diced
1 red onion, diced
4 tomatoes, diced
½ bunch fresh cilantro, chopped
3 serrano chiles, minced
    Juice of 5 lemons
    Salt and pepper to taste

In a large bowl, combine the jicama, onion, tomatoes and mix well.
Add the cilantro, chiles and lemon juice. Add salt and pepper to taste.

New Zealand Mussels In Cilantro & Serrano Cream Sauce

Serves 4
Preparation Time: 20 Minutes

12 New Zealand green lip mussels, cleaned
1 Tbsp. olive oil
2 Tbsps. butter
1 tsp. shallots, minced
1 tsp. garlic, minced
½ cup white wine
¼ cup heavy cream
1 tomato, chopped
½ red onion, chopped
1 Tbsp. fresh cilantro, chopped
1 serrano chile, minced
4 Tbsps. salsa fresca (recipe on page 115)

In a large sauté pan, heat the olive oil and butter. Add the shallots, garlic, mussels and wine. Cover and allow to cook over medium heat for 3 minutes or until mussels open. Remove the lid and discard any mussels that haven't opened.

Reduce the remaining liquid in the pan in half. Add cream, tomato, onion, cilantro and chile. Continue cooking for 2 minutes.

Remove the mussels from the pan and arrange them on a serving plate. Continue cooking the cream sauce until it is reduced by half.

Pour the sauce over the mussels and garnish with salsa fresca.

Cooking tip: This is a wonderful appetizer served with warm French bread.

Boston Clam Chowder

Preparation Time: 45 Minutes
Yield: One gallon

2 lbs. Manila clams, washed
2 qts. water
1 lb. clams, chopped
¼ cup oil
4 stalks celery, chopped
1¼ medium onions, chopped
¼ tsp. thyme
2 bay leaves, crushed
1 cup light roux (oil or butter mixed with flour in equal
  amounts over low heat)
4 medium potatoes, peeled, diced
2 qts. heavy cream or half and half

Place the Manila clams in a large pot with water and bring to a boil. When clam shells open, remove from pot, drain and discard the shells. Save the clam broth, set aside.

In another large pot, heat the oil and add the celery, onions, thyme and bay leaves. When vegetables and herbs are soft, add both the chopped clams and the clams. Add the clam broth. (Be careful not to add any sand that may have settled to the bottom of the broth).

Cook until the clams are tender. Add the roux, gently stirring it in. When the mixture is smooth, add the potatoes. Continue cooking for 15 minutes. As soon as the potatoes are cooked, add the cream or half and half, heating gently.

Cooking tip: This soup can be made in advance and refrigerates well without the cream. As you use it, add 2 cups of cream or half and half for each quart of clam base that you plan to serve.

Mixed Greens with Roasted Pecans and Honey Mustard Vinaigrette

Preparation Time: 15 Minutes
Yield: 2 cups salad dressing

- ¾ cup red wine vinegar
- 4 Tbsps. Dijon country-style mustard
- Salt to taste
- 1 Tbsp. honey
- 1 cup peanut oil
- 2 Tbsps. water
- Chilled mixed greens
- ¾ cup roasted pecans

In a quart jar or bottle, mix the vinegar and mustard, shake well. Add the seasonings and shake. Add the honey and continue to shake. Add the oil and water and shake until blended. Refrigerate.

On each of four individual plates, arrange a handful of chilled mixed greens. Top each salad with roasted pecans.

Dress each salad with the honey mustard vinaigrette.

Tilapia Cancun with Green Cashew Sauce

Serves 8

Preparation Time: 20 Minutes

- 1 cup cashews, roasted
- 2 cloves garlic
- 1 tsp. shallots
- 2 serrano chiles
- ¼ cup peanut oil
- 3 Tbsps. rice vinegar
- 1 Tbsp. water
- ½ bunch fresh cilantro
- Salt and pepper to taste
- Eight ¼ lb. Tilapia filets
- 2 Tbsps. paprika
- 1 Tsp. cayenne
- 1 lime, cut in half
- 1 cup Caribbean cole slaw (see recipe page 116)

In a food processor, puree the cashews, garlic, shallots and chiles. When the mixture has become a paste, add the oil and continue to puree. Add the vinegar and cilantro and puree until smooth. Season with salt and pepper. Set cashew sauce aside.

Rinse and dry the filets with a towel. Rub each side with a lime half and coat with paprika and cayenne. Sauté or flat grill the filets.

On individual plates, place each cooked filet on 1 Tbsp. of green cashew sauce. Top with 2 Tbsps. of Caribbean cole slaw. Serve immediately.

Caribbean Cole Slaw

Preparation Time: 10 Minutes (note refrigeration time)

½ head white cabbage, shredded
½ medium onion, diced
½ green bell pepper, diced
½ red bell pepper, diced
4 Serrano or jalapeño chiles, finely chopped
1 tsp. salt
⅛ Tbsp. black pepper
1 cup white vinegar
½ Tbsp. sugar

In a large bowl, combine the cabbage, onion, green and red bell pepper and chiles with the salt and black pepper. Stir in the vinegar and sugar.

Pack the cole slaw in a lidded container for at least 8 hours before serving, to allow the cabbage to "pickle".

Cooking tip: The Caribbean cole slaw will keep for a good week in the refrigerator, so it's a great make-ahead dish.

Key Lime Pie

Preparation Time: 30 Minutes (note refrigeration time)
Pre-heat oven to 350°

1¼ cups graham cracker crumbs
  6 Tbsps. sugar
  ¼ cup butter, melted
  1 tsp. cinnamon
  1 can condensed milk
  4 egg yolks
  2 Florida key limes, juice to equal 1 cup
  1 cup whipping cream

Combine graham cracker crumbs with 3 Tbsps. sugar. Add butter and cinnamon. Press crust mixture into pie plate. Bake at 350° for 12 minutes, then allow the crust to cool.

While crust is baking, prepare the filling by blending the condensed milk with the egg yolks. Add the lime juice and pour mixture into the cooled pie shell. Bake at 350° for 12 minutes to set the filling.

Whip the cream and 3 Tbsps. sugar together for the pie topping. Smooth it onto the top of the cooled pie. Refrigerate and serve chilled.

Cooking tip: If key limes are unavailable, use Bahamian or California limes.

GERNOT'S VICTORIA HOUSE RESTAURANT

AUSTRIAN CUISINE
649 Lighthouse Ave.
Pacific Grove
646-1477
Tuesday–Sunday 5:30–10PM
AVERAGE DINNER FOR TWO: $22

LOCATED IN THE old Hart Mansion, Gernot's Victoria House offers excellent European-type cuisine at moderate prices. The softly-lit fireside dining room conveys old-world elegance amid lace curtains and floral wallpaper.

The menu is innovative and interesting, offering entrees which include fresh wild boar from Carmel Valley, served in a red wine sauce with mushrooms and onions. The lamb Dijon is prepared with Dijon mustard, garlic and topped with a delicate polenta and salsa, and the famous Austrian Wiener schnitzel (lightly breaded young veal) is served with a lingonberry compote.

Owner-chef Gernot Leitzinger was the private chef for Prince Auersperg of Austria after he learned his cooking skills in Zurich, Davos and Amsterdam.

Menu for Four

Battered Mushrooms with Tartar Sauce
(Champignons Frits)
Breaded Veal
(Austrian Weiner Schnitzel)
Meringue Soufflé
(Salzburger Nockerl)

Battered Mushrooms with Tartar Sauce

Serves 4
Preparation Time: 15 Minutes

½ lb. fresh mushrooms
½ cup flour
2 eggs, beaten
1 cup breadcrumbs, sweet French bread
2 cups oil
Salt to taste
½ cup mayonnaise
1 dill pickle, chopped
Pickle Juice as needed
1 Tbsp. chives or green onions
Lemon wedge for garnish

Wash and quarter mushrooms. Bread them by dipping first in flour, then egg, then breadcrumbs.

Fry mushrooms in hot oil until golden brown. Remove with a strainer, letting excess oil drip off. Salt lightly.

In a medium bowl, combine the mayonnaise and dill pickle. If mixture seems too thick, add a little pickle juice or vinegar. Garnish with chives or green onions.

Serve mushrooms with tartar sauce and lemon wedges.

Original Austrian Wiener Schnitzel

Serves 4
Preparation Time: 45 Minutes

Four 5 oz. veal cutlets from loin or top round
Salt and white pepper to taste
1 tsp. fresh tarragon, chopped fine
2 eggs
¼ cup flour
1 cup bread crumbs, sweet French bread
1 cup oil
Browned melted butter, optional

Pound veal cutlets until very thin. Salt and pepper the meat and apply tarragon evenly.

In a medium-sized bowl, beat the eggs. Set aside. Place flour and bread crumbs each in separate plates.

Dip cutlets in flour, then in eggs, then bread crumbs. Shake off excess flour and crumbs.

Heat oil in frying pan until very hot. Fry cutlets on both side until golden brown. Remove and drain on paper towels.

Serve warm with browned butter poured over the cutlets.

Cooking tip: Traditional Austrian Schnitzels are served with a combination of salads: green, cucumber and potato salads.

Meringue Soufflé

Serves 4
Preparation Time: 15 Minutes
Pre-heat oven to 400°

1 Tbsp. butter, melted
¼ cup milk
6 egg whites
4 Tbsps. sugar
  Juice of half lemon
3 egg yolks
3 Tbsps. flour, sifted
  Powdered sugar as garnish
½ cup raspberry puree

Use a long ovenproof serving dish or platter with a ½" rim. Brush dish with the melted butter. Pour the milk into the dish.

Over high heat, bring the milk to a gentle boil. Remove from heat and set aside.

Beat egg whites with the sugar until very stiff. Blend in the lemon juice, egg yolks and flour. With a large wooden spoon, scoop the meringue mixture on top of the milk and form four individual peaks.

Bake in oven for 8 to 10 minutes or until golden brown.

Remove the soufflé from oven and sprinkle with powdered sugar. Serve immediately with the raspberry sauce on the side.

MELAC'S RESTAURANT

FRENCH
663 Lighthouse Ave.
Pacific Grove
375-1743
FRENCH CUISINE
Lunch Tuesday–Friday 11:30AM–2:00PM
Dinner Tuesday–Saturday 5:30PM–9:30PM

JANET MELAC, CORDON Bleu chef, and her husband, host Jacques Melac, have a roaring success on their hands, a pleasant neighborhood restaurant with reasonable prices and food so satisfying that people come from far and wide to eat here.

Their success is largely attributable to Melac's innovative French cooking style, offering simple dishes with light and elegant sauces. The sauces are mostly made-to-order with each dish.

The menu changes daily to ensure only the freshest organic ingredients are used. Specials include duck, lamb, veal, seafood, vegetarian creations and homemade desserts. The results are masterful presentations of such earthly delicacies as Jumbo Sea Scallops, seared in olive oil with a Coconut Basil Mussel Broth or Wild Mushroom Crepes with fresh Goat Cheese accompanying a Herbed Celery Root and Leek Compote.

Delightful entrees include the Tenderloin of Beef Roasted with Black Pepper and Cognac in a Herb and Spinach Sauce, Striped Bass sautéed with a sauce of Lemon and Herbs or the Veal Sweetbreads sautéed with Port and Madeira on a bed of Fettuccini tossed with White Truffle Oil.

There is a oneness at Melac's created by the overwhelming attraction of the food, the intimate setting of the restaurant and the friendly environment created by the guests who dine here.

Vegetable Terrine with a Curried Vinaigrette
Seafood Cassoulet
Truffle Cake

Curried Vinaigrette

Yield: One cup
Preparation Time: 5 Minutes

1 tsp. Dijon mustard
    Salt and pepper
2 Tbsps. red wine vinegar
2 Tbsps. sherry wine vinegar
2 Tbsps. beef stock
1 tsp. curry powder
1 cup olive oil

In a jar, shake to combine all the ingredients except the olive oil. Add the olive oil and shake again.

Serve the vinaigrette drizzled over the vegetable terrine. The recipe follows.

Vegetable Terrine

Preparation Time: 3 Hours (note refrigeration time)
Serves 8

  3 medium eggplants
    Olive oil
  2 large onions, sliced
  4 tomatoes, peeled, seeded, chopped
  4 red bell peppers, roasted, peeled, sliced
  ½ lb. shiitake mushrooms
  2 Tbsps. shallots, chopped
  3 garlic cloves, chopped
  2 eggs
    Butter
    Salt and pepper
    Curried vinaigrette (see previous recipe)

Slice the eggplant lengthwise into strips. Sprinkle with salt and pepper and drain in a colander.

Heat the olive oil in a skillet over medium heat and sauté the onion until soft. Add the tomato and cook until most of the moisture is gone. Add the roasted red bell peppers and cook until all the liquid is evaporated. Set aside.

Chop the cleaned shiitake mushrooms into small pieces and sauté them in olive oil with the shallots and garlic until dry. Season with salt and pepper. Set aside.

Sauté the eggplant in olive oil until soft. Drain off any excess oil.

In a food processor, combine the tomato mixture and the mushroom mixture. Add the egg, blending well. Season with salt and pepper.

Butter and line a terrine with plastic wrap. Layer the pureed vegetables and the eggplant strips. Cover with foil and bake in a water bath for 1½ hours at 400°.

Refrigerate for 24 hours before serving.

Serve with the curried vinaigrette.

Seafood Cassoulet

Serves 8
Preparation Time: 3 Hours

1 carrot, diced
1 rib celery, diced
1 small onion, diced
2 Tbsps. olive oil
2 cups navy beans, soaked overnight in water
8 cups prawn stock (recipe follows)
   Salt and pepper to taste

In a large pot, sauté the carrots, celery and onions in olive oil. Add the drained beans and the prawn stock. Cover and simmer until the beans are tender. It might be necessary to add stock so they do not dry out, depending on the freshness of the beans. Season with salt and pepper. The cooking time is approximately 1 to 1½ hours.

Add the smoked salmon sausages and the scallop sausages, recipe follows, to the beans, 15 minutes before serving.

Prawn Stock

4 garlic cloves
2 carrots
4 ribs celery
1 leek
3 Tbsps. olive oil
3 lbs. prawns
4 Tbsps. tomato paste
1 bunch tarragon
1 bunch parsley
2 cups white wine
2 cups cognac
Water

Chop all the vegetables and herbs roughly, then sauté the vegetables in a large pot with olive oil. Add the prawns and sauté for 5 minutes. Add the tomato paste, wine and brandy. Add water to just cover the prawn mixture. Add the herbs. Bring stock to a boil and simmer for 20 minutes. Strain out the solids before using the stock.

Smoked Salmon Sausages

Yield: 8 Sausages
Preparation Time: 5 Minutes

1½ lbs. fresh salmon
½ lb. cold smoked salmon
½ cup cream
1 Tbsp. dill or fennel, chopped
Salt and pepper
8 sausage casings

In a food processor, combine both salmons, cream, herbs, salt and pepper, blending until smooth. Fill the sausage casings to make 8 sausages. Refrigerate until ready to use.

Scallop Sausages

Yield: 8 Sausages
Preparation Time: 5 Minutes

2 lbs. sea scallops, muscle removed
½ cup cream
1 Tbsp. fresh tarragon, chopped
Salt and pepper
8 sausage casings

In a food processor, combine the scallops, cream, tarragon, salt and pepper, blending until smooth. Fill the sausage casings to make 8 sausages. Refrigerate until ready to use.

Truffle Cake

Serves 8
Preparation Time: One Hour (note refrigeration time)
Pre-heat oven to 375°

  10 oz. good quality chocolate
   5 eggs
1½ cups cream, whipped
    Cocoa powder
    Butter
    Raspberry puree, optional

Break the chocolate into small pieces, and melt in the top of a double boiler over simmering water, stirring frequently. Remove the pan from the heat and set it aside.

In a mixing bowl, beat the eggs together. Fold the warm chocolate into the whipped eggs. Fold in the whipped cream.

Pour the batter into a buttered cake pan and smooth the top with a rubber spatula. Set the cake pan in a larger baking pan, and fill the larger pan with enough hot water to come halfway up the side of the cake pan. Place the pans in the oven, and bake at 375° until a toothpick inserted in the center of the cake comes out clean, about 30 to 40 minutes. Transfer the cake to a wire rack and allow the cake to cool. Then refrigerate it, still in the pan, until firm, 6 hours or overnight.

Unmold before serving. This cake is often served with a raspberry puree, espresso or vanilla sauce.

OLD BATH HOUSE

CALIFORNIA CUISINE
620 Ocean View Blvd.
Pacific Grove
375-5195
Dinner Monday–Friday 5PM–10:30PM
Saturday 4PM–11PM
Sunday 3PM–10:30PM
Bar open 4PM–12 Midnight
AVERAGE DINNER FOR TWO: $70

THE OLD BATH HOUSE, located at Lovers Point Park, offers some of the most beautiful, romantic, ocean-side dining anywhere in the world. This is the site of the original bathhouse which stood as a famous California landmark in the 1800's.

The Old Bath House continues to earn extraordinary acclaim. Here, guests enjoy superb California cuisine, fine wines and an ambiance graced by rich leather furniture, hand-carved woods and etched glass.

An adjoining 30-seat Victorian bar and lounge provides a cozy setting for a rendezvous with friends for cocktails.

Old Bath House
R E S T A U R A N T

Menu for Six

Smoked Pheasant & Duck Carpaccio
Fruit of the Sea Salad
with Mango Vinaigrette
Veal Monarch
Amaretto Tiramisu with Espresso Sauce

Smoked Pheasant & Duck Carpaccio

Serves 6
Preparation Time: 20 Minutes

1 cantaloupe melon, sliced lengthwise
1 honeydew melon, sliced lengthwise
1 whole smoked pheasant, skin removed
1 smoked duck breast, skin removed
1 cup walnut oil
½ cup champagne vinegar
  Salt and white pepper to taste
1 cup walnut halves
1 Tbsp. chives

On a large plate, arrange the sliced melons in alternating colors, fanned out.

Slice the meat off the pheasant and duck lengthwise and fan over the melons.

Prepare the dressing by combining the walnut oil and vinegar. Season with salt and pepper.

Drizzle dressing over the pheasant, duck and melons. Garnish with walnuts and chives.

Fruit of the Sea Salad

Serves 6
Preparation Time: 15 Minutes

12 large shrimp
12 jumbo scallops
 3 cups mixture baby lettuces and herbs
    Red cherry tomatoes
    Yellow pear tomatoes
 1 cucumber, sliced
 1 bunch radishes, sliced

Cook the shrimp and scallops individually in boiling salted water. Rinse and set aside to cool.

Wash and dry lettuce and arrange on individual salad plates. Garnish with both the red and yellow tomatoes, cucumbers and radishes.

Place 2 shrimp and 2 scallops on top of the salad and drizzle with the mango vinaigrette.

Mango Vinaigrette

¾ cup peanut oil
 1 cup mango puree
¼ cup white wine
    Salt to taste

In a blender, slowly add the peanut oil to the mango puree. Thin dressing with white wine. Season with salt.

Veal Monarch

Serves 6
Preparation Time: One hour

6 medium artichokes
Juice of 1 lemon
4 garlic cloves, chopped
2½ lbs. veal top round
2 Tbsps. butter
2 Tbsps. peanut oil
1 cup cognac
1½ pt. heavy cream
2 shallots, chopped
½ cup pine nuts
1 bunch Italian parsley, chopped
2 baby leeks, diced medium

Clean artichokes and cut into eighths. Blanch in enough water to cover, with lemon and 2 cloves garlic. Cook approximately 45 minutes, but start to check for doneness after 35 minutes. Peel off outer leaves and remove fibrous center. Reserve.

Cut veal into 7 oz. portions and pound thin. In two large skillets, using butter and peanut oil in each skillet, sear off veal. Place veal on a separate pan and keep warm.

In the two skillets, add ½ of the cognac to each, burning off all the alcohol. Add cream and reduce.

Slice remaining garlic and add to the sauce the shallots, pine nuts, parsley, leeks and reserved artichokes. Continue to reduce.

Pour off all meat drippings into the sauce and blend to a creamy consistency. Serve immediately.

Amaretto Tiramisu

Serves 6
Preparation Time: 30 Minutes

22 Ladyfingers
1 cup strong espresso, cooled
½ cup Amaretto
5 eggs, separated
½ cup sugar
1½ cups Mascarpone cheese
½ cup bittersweet chocolate, chopped
Cocoa powder

Lightly soak half the Ladyfingers in the espresso and Amaretto and set aside.

Mix egg yolks and sugar until lemony. Add Mascarpone and mix until smooth. Set aside.

Whip egg whites until stiff. Fold into Mascarpone mixture.

Place the espresso-soaked Ladyfingers in a 10'x6" pan 3" deep and put half the Mascarpone mixture on top. Sprinkle half the chocolate on top of the Mascarpone. Repeat layering procedure with remaining Ladyfingers, Mascarpone and chocolate to total two layers. Dust lightly with cocoa powder.

Cover with aluminum foil and refrigerate for a minimum of one hour or overnight.

Serve with Espresso Sauce, on following page.

Espresso Sauce

Preparation Time: 10 Minutes

  1 **cup milk**
  1 **cup heavy cream**
  1 **tsp. vanilla extract**
  6 **egg yolks**
½ **cup sugar**
  1 **Tbsp. coffee extract**
  1 **Tbsp. coffee liqueur**

Bring the milk and cream to a boil with the vanilla extract. Slowly mix in the egg yolks and sugar, stirring continuously until smooth and lemony in color.

Flavor with the coffee extract and coffee liqueur.

Spoon warm espresso sauce over the Amaretto tiramisu.

PASTA MIA RESTAURANT

ITALIAN CUISINE
481 Lighthouse Ave.
Pacific Grove, CA 93950
375-7709
Dinner nightly 5PM
Closed Monday
AVERAGE DINNER FOR TWO: $35

As YOU CLIMB the steps of this quaint Victorian house, you will be treated to the aroma of fresh garlic and herbs. Venture through the doors to view the colorful variety of appealing antipastos displayed on the nearby table.

The extremely personable owner, Maureen Signorella, decided to open a trattoria, as opposed to a ristorante, upon returning from a two year stint in Italy. She wanted to create her own "bella Italia" here in Northern California.

That was seven years ago, and actually nothing has really changed for her, except that instead of cooking and eating with a few people, she does it for a 100 or so people.

The food is prepared fresh each day by chef Daniel Vitanza with either Maureen or sister Kathy at the door to greet you.

pasta mia

Menu for Four

Radicchio Walnut Salad
Chicken Puttanesca with Polenta
Zabaglione Freddo

Radicchio Walnut Salad

Serves 4
Preparation Time: 15 Minutes

2 pears
1 large head radicchio
½ cup walnuts
1 large fennel
¼ cup olive oil
Salt and pepper to taste

Wash radicchio and drain. Tear into bite-sized pieces.

Quarter pears, core and cut crosswise. Add sliced fennel and walnuts.

Toss with olive oil, salt and pepper to taste.

Chill and serve.

Chicken Puttanesca with Polenta

Serves 4
Prepartion Time: 45 Minutes
Pre-heat oven to 350°

½ Tbsp. sliced garlic
½ cup calamata olives
4 anchovies
½ tsp. red chile peppers
2 Tbsps. capers
3 cups tomato sauce
2½ lbs. chicken pieces
¼ cup olive oil
1 cup polenta, cooked

Saute garlic, olives, anchovies, peppers and capers in 2 Tbsps. olive oil. Add the tomato sauce and simmer for 2 minutes. Set aside.

Pan fry the chicken pieces in remaining olive oil for approximately 15 minutes or until tender. Drain the oil and pat the chicken dry.

Place chicken in a shallow baking pan and cover with the Puttanesca sauce. Cover the chicken and bake for 15 minutes at 350°. Serve the chicken and sauce over the polenta.

This Puttanesca Sauce is also excellent over linguini.

Zabaglione Freddo

Serves 4
Preparation Time: 30 Minutes

8 egg yolks
1 cup granulated sugar
½ cup Florio dry Marsala wine
   Orange zest
2 pts. fresh berries
   Fresh mint leaves

Mix the egg yolks, sugar, wine and orange zest in a double boiler. Begin whisking the ingredients, making sure the water underneath does not come to a full boil.

The mixture will become light and fluffy in approximately 20 minutes.

Zabaglione is cooked when the mixture looks like whipped cream.

Chill for approximately one hour.

Pour over fresh berries in individual dishes and garnish with mint leaves

This zabaglione can be prepared the day before and refrigerated.

PEPPERS MEXI CALI CAFE

MEXICAN/LATIN AMERICAN CUISINE
170 Forest Ave.
Pacific Grove, CA 93950
373-6892
Lunch and dinner daily 11:30AM–10PM
Sunday 4–10PM
Closed Tuesday
AVERAGE DINNER FOR TWO: $25

WITHOUT A DOUBT, Peppers is one of the locals' most popular restaurants—and with good reason.

Specializing in Mexican and Latin American cuisine, Peppers takes the genre beyond the greasy tacos and refried beans. Peppers presents dishes that are fresh and simply prepared—with a great deal of imagination.

Seafood variations are featured daily and black beans offer a welcome change from the usual pinto beans. The traditional dishes are delicious; the innovative dishes are surprisingly good.

Peppers offers a warm, friendly atmosphere, an extensive wine list and an excellent selection of imported beers.

Open for lunch and dinner.

> ### Menu for Four
>
> *Steamed Clams and Mussels*
> *with Mixed Bell Pepper Medley*
> *Grilled Sea Scallop Salad with Cilantro Vinaigrette*
> *Yucatan Prawns with Black Beans and Spanish Rice*
> *Salsa Cruda and Avocado Salsa*

Steamed Mussels and Clams with Mixed Bell Pepper Medley

Serves 4
Preparation Time: 30 Minutes

12 Littleneck or Manila clams
12 New Zealand mussels (may substitute East Coast mussels)
1 Bermuda onion, sliced
3 tomatoes diced
1 red, yellow and green bell pepper sliced
4 cloves garlic, sliced
1 cup white wine
Juice of 2 limes
½ stick butter
Cilantro sprigs for garnish
Tortillas

Clean and scrub mussels and clams. Use only the ones that are closed tightly.

Combine wine, lime juice and butter in a large sauce pan over medium heat. Add all vegetables and garlic and cook 3-5 minutes or until limp. Add clams and mussels, cover and simmer untill shells open. Discard any that don't open.

Pour into individual bowls and garnish with cilantro sprigs. Serve with warmed tortillas for dipping and scooping.

Grilled Sea Scallop Salad with Cilantro Vinaigrette

Serves 4
Preparation Time: 20 Minutes

Salad

1 lb. fresh sea scallops
1 each red leaf, romaine and butter lettuce
3 sliced tomatoes
  Black olives, pitted
3 scallions

Vinaigrette

2 Tbsps. white wine
2 Tbsps. orange juice
2 Tbsps. fresh lime juice
2 Tbsps. rice wine vinegar
6 Tbsps. olive oil
½ cup chopped cilantro
  Pinch salt, sugar and pepper
1 clove garlic, minced

Combine all ingredients for the vinaigrette and mix well. Toss cleaned lettuce, torn into bite-sized pieces with the vinaigrette.

Grill or broil scallops until they are opaque in the center.

Garnish lettuce with tomatoes, olives, scallions and top with warm grilled scallops.

Yucatan Prawns

Serves 4
Preparation Time: 30 Minutes

2 lbs. medium-large prawns shelled, deveined and butterflied
1 red onion, diced
2 tomatoes, diced
2 chiles, diced
1 red bell pepper, diced
¼ cup cilantro, chopped
   Juice of 2 oranges
   Juice of 3 limes
¼ cup white wine
¼ cup fish stock
1 tsp. oregano
½ tsp. salt

Combine all ingredients except the prawns in a large saucepan.
Cook over medium heat for 10 minutes. Add the prawns and cook for 5
minutes.

Arrange prawns in individual bowls with portions of vegetables
and broth. Garnish with chopped cilantro. Offer with Salsa Cruda or
Avocado Salsa.

Black Beans

Serves 8
Preparation Time: 3 Hours

2 lbs. black beans
1 onion, chopped
1 bell pepper, chopped
3 cloves garlic, chopped
   Bay leaf
2 Tbsps. cumin
3 Tbsps. chile pepper

Sort beans for dirt and pebbles and wash well. Place in a large pot with all ingredients and cover with water. On high heat, bring beans to a boil, reduce heat and cook until tender, about 2 hours. Add water as necessary to avoid drying out.

Salsa Cruda

Preparation Time: 5 Minutes

5 large tomatoes, chopped
1 onion
1 bunch of cilantro, chopped
2 serrano or jalapeño chiles
   Juice of one lime

Mix the above ingredients for a zesty salsa.

Spanish Rice

Serves 8
Preparation Time: One Hour

2 cups long grain rice
2 tomatoes, diced
1 cup tomato juice
1 onion, diced
1 cup green chiles, diced
1 Tbsp. garlic, minced
3 Tbsps. olive oil
2 cups water
2 Tbsps. salt

Saute all vegetables in olive oil in a large sauce pan over medium heat. Add rice, water, tomato juice and bring to a boil, stirring continuously. Cover tightly and reduce heat to very low. Cook until done, approximately 30 minutes.

Avocado Salsa

Preparation Time: 5 Minutes

5 large tomatoes, chopped
1 onion, chopped
1 bunch of cilantro
2 serrano or jalapeño chiles
   Juice of one lime
¼ cup orange juice
1 Tbsp. rice wine vinegar
2 Tbsps. olive oil
3 avocados, chopped

Blend the above ingredients together for a truly unique salsa.

TASTE CAFE & BISTRO

MEDITERRANEAN CUISINE
1199 Forest Ave #5
Pacific Grove
655-0324
Lunch Tuesday–Sunday 11:30AM–3PM
Dinner 5PM–9PM
Friday & Saturday 5PM–11PM
Closed Mondays
AVERAGE DINNER FOR TWO: $25

FROM THE MOMENT Taste Cafe and Bistro opened, the restaurant has become a local favorite. Taste is one of those cozy neighborhood places that makes it a pleasure to eat out. And the delicious food always comes at a remarkably low price.

This small restaurant with its cappuccino-wine bar is classically decorated in a rustic Mediterranean style. Seating is at white linen tables with richly upholstered banquettes. The place sparkles. The restaurant is clean, fresh and well polished.

Dining guests enjoy watching chef/owners Sylvia Medina and Paulo Kautz in their open kitchen, creating each dish with attention to detail. The menu offers a selection of contemporary cooking with French and Italian flavors. An assortment of fresh desserts completes a perfect meal.

CAFE & BISTRO

Menu for Six

Italian Quesadillas with Tomato-Basil Salsa
Tuscan White Bean Soup
Chicken Breasts with Artichokes and Fettuccine
Strawberries in Balsamic Vinegar with Vanilla Gelato

Tomato-Basil Salsa

Serves 6
Preparation Time: 10 Minutes

5 medium tomatoes, peeled, seeded, diced
1 small red onion, finely diced
½ bunch basil leaves, chopped
1 Tbsp. champagne vinegar
2 tsps. extra virgin olive oil
2 garlic cloves, minced
   Salt and pepper to taste

Combine all ingredients in a large mixing bowl. Adjust seasonings to taste.

Serve with the Italian quesadillas.

Italian Quesadillas

Serves 6
Preparation Time: 15 Minutes

 2 **large eggplants, sliced ¼″ thick**
   Olive oil
   Salt and pepper
12 **flour tortillas**
 3 **cups smoked mozzarella cheese, grated**
 1 **cup sun-dried tomatoes, quartered**

Sprinkle salt and pepper over eggplant and brush with olive oil. Grill eggplant on both sides or broil in oven. Cut eggplant into wide strips or triangles.

Lay six tortillas on counter and top each one with eggplant, smoked mozzarella cheese and sun-dried tomatoes. Cover each one with the remaining tortillas.

Sauté each quesadilla in hot oil quickly on both sides, so as not to burn the tortilla. Place on paper towels to blot excess oils.

Place on 6 individual serving plates, cutting each quesadilla into six triangles. Spoon the fresh tomato-basil salsa on top before serving.

Tuscan White Bean Soup

Serves 6
Preparation Time: 1½ hours (note soaking time for beans)

1½ cups onion, coarsely chopped
 2 smoked ham hocks
 2 Tbsps. unsalted butter
 8 cups chicken stock
 1 cup dry white beans, soaked overnight
 4 whole garlic cloves
¼ tsp. fresh thyme, chopped
 5 tomatoes, peeled, seeded, chopped
 1 small Napa cabbage, coarsely chopped
   Salt and pepper to taste
   Parmesan cheese

In a large soup pot, sauté onions and ham hocks in butter until the onions are golden in color. Add chicken stock, white beans, garlic cloves and thyme.

Bring soup to a boil, then simmer for 1 hour or more until beans are tender. Remove ham hocks from soup and dice ham off the bones. Discard bones and add the ham back into the soup. Add tomatoes, cabbage and a little water, if necessary. Simmer 10–15 minutes. Season with salt and pepper.

Ladle into 6 hot soup bowls and top with freshly shaved Parmesan cheese.

Chicken Breasts with Artichokes

Serves 6
Preparation Time: 45 Minutes

12 chicken breasts, boned
    Salt and pepper
¼ cup flour
 4 Tbsps. olive oil
 1 medium onion, diced small
 4 small garlic cloves, minced
 1 lb. mushrooms, sliced
 1 cup dry sherry
 6 medium tomatoes, peeled, quartered
 2 jars marinated artichokes, drained, 6 oz. each
 1 tsp. oregano, dried
 2 tsps. basil, dried

Salt and pepper chicken breasts. Coat in flour, shaking off excess, then sauté in 2 Tbsps. olive oil for 5–7 minutes on each side. Transfer to serving platter and keep warm

Prepare the sauce by sautéing onions in 2 Tbsps. olive oil until transparent. Add the garlic and cook until golden. Add mushrooms and stir constantly until liquid evaporates. Add dry sherry, tomatoes, artichokes, oregano and basil. Lower heat and cook approximately 20 minutes uncovered. Adjust seasonings to taste.

Pour sauce over chicken breasts and serve.

Cooking tip: Fettuccine is a wonderful accompaniment to this dish.

Strawberries in Balsamic Vinegar with Vanilla Gelato

Serves 6
Preparation Time: 10 Minutes

½ **cup sugar**
8 **Tbsps. balsamic vinegar**
4 **Tbsps. lemon juice**
  Pinch fresh black pepper
4 **baskets strawberries, quartered**
  Chocolate for shaving
  Vanilla gelato
  Mint leaves for garnish

Combine the sugar, vinegar, lemon and pepper. Toss the strawberries into this mixture and marinate for 5 minutes.

Place strawberries in serving bowls. With a potato peeler, shave chocolate on top of the berries. Top with vanilla gelato and garnish with mint.

VITO'S ITALIAN RESTAURANT

ITALIAN CUISINE
1180 Forest Hills Shopping Center
Pacific Grove
375-3070
Dinner Sunday–Tuesday 5PM–10:PM
AVERAGE DINNER FOR TWO: $25

VITO'S ITALIAN RESTAURANT offers excellent food in an unpretentious setting, with Italian-style hospitality. The staff strives to make you feel like a neighbor, whether you are a local or a visitor to the Peninsula.

This authentic Italian kitchen offers specialties such as fettucine alla puttanesca (fresh tomatoes, anchovy, capers and black olives combined with olive oil and fresh pasta), scampi alla romana (prawns in a champagne cream sauce) and homemade cannolis.

Vito's is a cozy, upscale haven where hearty conversation, great food and wine and expert service prevail. A secret place that local residents would prefer to keep to themselves.

Buon appetito.

VITO'S ITALIAN RESTAURANT

Menu for Four

Eggplant Parmigiana
Cannelloni
Ice Cream Torte

Eggplant Parmigiana

Serves 4
Preparation Time: 10 Minutes
Pre-heat oven to 325°

  1 eggplant, peeled, sliced thin
¼ cup olive oil
    Salt to taste
  1 cup tomato sauce
  1 Tbsp. fresh basil, chopped
½ cup Parmesan cheese, grated

In olive oil, sauté the eggplant until brown. Drain and salt. Place the eggplant in a oiled casserole dish.

Top eggplant with tomato sauce and basil. Sprinkle the cheese over the tomato sauce and bake for 10-15 minutes.

Serve warm.

Cannelloni

Serves 4
Preparation Time: 25 Minutes.
Pre-heat oven to 325°

2 cups ground veal
3 cloves garlic, sliced
½ onion, sliced
1 carrot, sliced
2 bunches spinach
2 cups milk
¼ stick butter
5 Tbsps. flour
1 tsp. nutmeg
1 cup mozzarella, grated fine
1 cup Parmesan, grated fine
Cannelloni pasta, cooked
2 cups tomato sauce

In a sauté pan, cook the veal with the garlic, onion and carrots until done. Drain and set aside.

Clean spinach and remove stems. Cook over medium heat and drain excess water.

Prepare a bechamel sauce (white sauce) by bringing the milk to a simmer. Add the butter and slowly stir in the flour. Season with nutmeg. Continue to simmer, stirring until thick, about 10 minutes.

Add the veal mixture, bechamel sauce and both cheeses to the spinach, stir thoroughly.

Stuff the veal spinach mixture into the cannelloni shells and place in a well-oiled baking pan. Top with tomato sauce.

Cook for 15 minutes or until warm.

Ice Cream Torte

Serves 8
Preparation Time: 45 Minutes (note refrigeration time)
Pre-heat oven to 350°

6 eggs
1½ cups flour
1½ cups sugar
3 tsps. baking powder
½ cup Kahlua liqueur
¼ pint hazelnut ice cream
¼ pint cappucino or coffee ice cream
1 pt. heavy cream, whipped

In a large bowl, separate the egg whites and beat until stiff. Slowly blend in the flour, sugar, baking powder and egg yolks, mixing well.

Pour the batter into a buttered 9-inch round cake pan or 9 × 13-inch sheet pan. Bake for 30 minutes or until a knife inserted in the center of the cake comes out clean.

Cool cake and remove from baking pan. Slice cake into 1-inch squares.

In a large loaf pan, place one layer of the cake squares. Sprinkle the top of the cake squares with Kahlua.

Top the cake with a layer of the hazelnut ice cream and a layer of the cappucino or coffee ice cream.

Top the ice cream layers with whipped cream.

On top of the cream mixture place the remaining cake squares. Again, sprinkle the cake top with Kahlua.

Freeze torte for 1 hour or until frozen. Warm to room temperature for 10 minutes. Run knife around pan edges, then invert the torte onto a plate.

Serve with remaining whipped cream as garnish.

POSH PLAYGROUND
PEBBLE BEACH

DOÑA MARIA del Carmen Barreto was a bit of a romantic. She owned about 4,000 acres of an old Mexican land grant, El Pescadero.

It was a lovely piece of land, facing the Pacific Ocean on one side and bordered by Pacific Grove, Monterey and Carmel. But Doña Maria felt isolated in her country home. She wanted to join the fiestas and "look out on life and romance" in Monterey. So, in 1840, she sold El Pescadero for $500.

Today, that tract of land comprises most of the 5,300 acres of Pebble Beach. In fact, the Lodge at Pebble Beach now stands on part of El Pescadero (Spanish for the Fishing Place).

The extraordinarily beautiful land changed hands several times. Monterey land baron David Jacks bought the land, then sold it in 1879 for $35,000 to the Big Four railroad barons: Charles Crocker, Leland Stanford, Mark Hopkins and Collis Huntington.

THESE FOUR, who gained fame for their part in building the transcontinental railroad, formed the Pacific Improvement Company. At Crocker's urging, the company in 1880 built the fabulous Del Monte Hotel in Monterey. That luxurious hotel, which introduced tourism to the Monterey Peninsula, was so avant-garde that it boasted a telephone in every room. That was astonishing in 1880.

Early visitors tour the breathtaking 17 Mile Drive.

THE DEL MONTE Hotel was the original starting point of the 17 Mile Drive that led horse-drawn carriages through Monterey and Pacific Grove to the remote, wild country of Pebble Beach. Today, the old hotel is part of the Naval Postgraduate School and 17 Mile Drive is confined to 12 miles in Del Monte Forest, the proper name of the area commonly known as Pebble Beach.

THE EARLY TOURISTS were captivated by the wonderful coastline of rugged cliffs and sparkling blue water, the haunting, twisted Monterey cypress trees, and the beauty of the woodland trails. Many stopped to picnic at a particular beach full of shiny pebbles.

Another popular stop was at the Lone Cypress, a rare species of tree indigenous to the Del Monte Forest and Point Lobos. The Lone Cypress, bravely clinging to a rocky headland, has become perhaps the most photographed tree in the world. Robert Louis Stevenson called the wind-twisted cypresses "ghosts fleeing before the wind."

Enter Samuel Finley Brown Morse, a recent graduate of Yale University and grand-nephew of Samuel Finley Breese Morse, inventor of the telegraph.

THE AMBITIOUS young man became manager of the Pacific Improvement Company's properties. By that time, Pacific's assets included two run-down hotels, a golf course badly in need of repair, large tracts of undeveloped land and a sand mine. Everything except the sand mine was losing money.

Morse was convinced that the holding would become profitable, but the Big Four wanted to liquidate. They gave Morse, not yet 30, the opportunity to meet their asking price.

With help from San Francisco financier Herbert Fleishhacker, Morse came up with the $1.3 million asking price and Del Monte Properties Co. was formed in 1919.

MORSE HAD TWO key visions for Del Monte Forest: he considered it important that the forest be kept intact and he envisioned a series of golf courses.

Morse threw out a plan to build a large number of homes on small lots. And at a time when there were only 400 golf courses in America, he brought in golf pro Jack Neville to design the Pebble Beach championship golf course in 1918. Then he built two 18-hole courses, the Monterey Peninsula Country Club and the exclusive Cypress Point Golf Club. Thus began a Pebble Beach golf mecca that now includes Spyglass Hill, Poppy Hills and the Links at Spanish Bay.

BECAUSE LARGE NUMBERS of small homes were ruled out, more opulent homes, mansions and small palaces began to pop up in those pre-Depression days.

Posh homes included marble pillars, towers above the cliffs, gold plumbing fixtures, priceless antiques and art, swimming pools and, of course, high walls with imposing gates to keep out the curious.

One of the most imposing of the early mansions was the Macomber house, constructed in 1917. The huge structure was built almost entirely of logs. The estate covered more than 75 acres, overlooking Carmel Bay.

The living room, which also served as a ballroom, contained 1,800 square feet, larger than many modern homes. The dining room was 30 feet long, 30 feet wide and 30 feet high. Largely unoccupied for most of its existence, the log mansion burned down in 1977.

ANOTHER PEBBLE BEACH home along 17 Mile Drive is a scaled-down version of a Middle Eastern palace, complete with marble columns and a sand-bottomed swimming pool built on a ledge halfway down the cliff. The pool boasts radiant-heated sand to protect chilly toes on those foggy days so common along the coast.

One still hears stories about another of the forest's early buildings. It is said that the Canary Cottage was once a gambling casino that catered only to invited guests in evening clothes. What makes the tales of an exclusive casino more plausible is the pre-Depression influx of Hollywood types. The exclusivity of a posh Pacific playground between Hollywood and San Francisco drew many from the film colony to dress up for polo matches and elegant parties in a discreet setting.

AND BECAUSE Pebble Beach is so conscious of privacy (the forest has its own security force and charges an admission fee at the entry gates), tidbits of lore seem all the more delicious. Accounts from the turn of the century even speak of smugglers using Stillwater Cove to bring in opium, sake and illegal aliens. It is believed that the opium and sake ended up in the Chinatown that flourished for a time at Pacific Grove and Monterey.

ON DECEMBER 20, 1941, an unarmed American tanker ship, the Agwiworld, was attacked by a Japanese submarine off Cypress Point. The tanker managed to outmaneuver the sub and escape, but the incident resulted in a flood of wide-eyed accounts from the ship's crew and from astonished golfers who witnessed the attack while playing the Cypress Point course.

No account of Pebble Beach would be complete without Bing Crosby, who hosted his National Pro-Am Golf Championship, the Crosby Clambake, in Pebble Beach. Now called the AT&T Pebble Beach National Pro-Am, the tournament draws thousands of spectators each year in January. The tournament draws a wide range of sports figures, show biz personalities, and amateur and professional golfers to the Pebble Beach, Cypress Point and Spyglass Hill courses. For many fans, this is their only chance to see the exclusive courses.

Other prestigious events in Pebble Beach include the Concours d'Elegance, a classic car show, the Pebble Beach Summer Horse Show and the Pebble Beach Dressage Championships, the Del Monte Kennel Club Dog Show and the National Rugby Championships.

PEBBLE BEACH DATEBOOK: Spaulding Pro-Am Golf, January; AT&T National Pro-Am, January; Polo Matches, April; Del Monte Kennel Club Dog Show, May; National Rugby Tournament, May; Spring Horse Show, May; Concours d'Elegance, August; NCGA Amateur Golf, August; Summer Horse Show, August; California Challenge Polo Match, September; Almaden Senior Tennis Tournament, September; California Women's Amateur Golf, December.

Bing Crosby, originator of the National Pro-Am Golf Championship, drew big crowds and occasionally big clouds.

THE BAY CLUB RESTAURANT

NORTHERN ITALIAN CUISINE
The Inn at Spanish Bay
2700 17-Mile Drive
Pebble Beach, CA 93953
647-7500
Dinner nightly 6PM–10PM
AVERAGE DINNER FOR TWO: $80

ON PICTURESQUE 17-Mile Drive, The Bay Club overlooks the Spanish Bay golf course and white sand beaches. Pebble Beach's latest restaurant features outstanding Northern Italian cuisine with an emphasis on fresh meats and vegetables and exceptional seafood. Chef Drew Previti studied under the Master Chef Gualtiero Marchesi, the first Italian restaurant to receive three stars from the Michelin Guide. Discerning travelers come year-round to enjoy the world-renowned Pebble Beach experience, in which fine dining plays a starring role.

Accommodations include 270 luxurious rooms and suites in an elegant and almost indulgent sense of retreat. Each room has its own fireplace, custom-made furnishings and four-poster beds topped with quilted down comforters. Most guest rooms offer a private balcony or patio, and in every case views are magnificent.

Gracious hospitality, exemplary service and unequaled dining amid scenic grandeur of extravagant proportions.

Menu for Four

Salmon al Piatto
Saffron Risotto
Lobster with Asparagus in Red Wine Sauce
White Coffee Mousse

Salmon al Piatto

Serves 4
Preparation Time: 10 Minutes

1 lb. filet of salmon
4 tomatoes
2 Tbsps. tarragon, chopped
2 Tbsps. extra virgin olive oil
¼ tsp. fine salt
¼ tsp. coarse salt

Blanch and peel tomatoes, then dice small. In a mixing bowl, combine the tomatoes with the tarragon, olive oil and fine salt. Set aside.

Slice salmon into 4 thin filets and pound flat. Place salmon on a heat-resistant serving plate and top with the tomato mixture.

Broil for 2 minutes or until medium-rare. Sprinkle salmon with coarse salt and serve.

Saffron Risotto

Serves 4
Preparation Time: 30 Minutes

1 cup risotto	½ cup white wine
¼ cup butter	½ cup white beef broth or
2 Tbsps. fine dried onion	chicken stock
Pinch of saffron	2 Tbsps. Parmesan cheese

In a saucepan or skillet, over medium heat, combine the risotto with half the butter, dried onion and saffron. Stir continuously until the risotto is lightly toasted. Add the wine and reduce until risotto is dry. Slowly add the broth while stirring the risotto. Add the remaining butter and Parmesan cheese before serving.

Lobster with Asparagus in Red Wine Sauce

Serves 4
Preparation Time: 30 Minutes

4 lobsters, 1½ lbs. each	¼ cup olive oil
¼ cup olive oil	1 carrot, chopped
¾ cup butter	1 onion, chopped
1 bottle red wine	24 asparagus, blanched
1 cup port wine	

Clean and cut lobsters, drizzle with olive oil and pan roast in 425° oven for 7 minutes. Remove meat and reserve carcass.

Combine the lobster shells with the carrot and onion over medium heat in a sauté pan until vegetables are soft, about 15 minutes. Deglaze with wine and port over medium heat until liquid is reduced by ⅓. Strain sauce from vegetables and shells. Gently stir in butter.

To serve, arrange asparagus on serving plate, top with lobster meat and drizzle with sauce.

White Coffee Mousse

Serves 4
Preparation Time: 45 Minutes (note refrigeration time)

1 pt. milk
½ cup coffee beans
7 eggs, separated
½ cup Crème De Cacao Bianco
1 cup cream, whipped
½ Tbsp. Knox gelatin or 3 gelatin leaves
¼ cup sugar
    Orange peel, julienned

Over high heat, bring the milk and coffee beans to a boil. Remove from heat and cool 20 minutes. Gently stir in yolks and sugar. Return to medium heat, stirring continuously until mixture thickens. Add gelatin and cool in an ice bath.

Whip egg whites until stiff. Set aside.

When mousse is cool, strain through a sieve and add the liqueur and whipped cream. Gently fold in the egg whites and pour into a mold. Refrigerate for 4 hours or until firm.

To serve, unmold onto orange sauce and decorate with julienne orange peel.

Orange Sauce

1 cup sugar
2 qts. orange juice
2 Tbsps. Grand Marnier
2 Tbsps. corn starch

Cook sugar over medium heat until color is a light caramel color. Deglaze with orange juice and bring to a boil. Add corn starch, strain, and add the Grand Marnier.

CLUB XIX

FRENCH CUISINE
The Lodge at Pebble Beach
17 Mile Drive
Pebble Beach, CA 93953
625-8519
Lunch daily 11:30AM–4PM
Dinner nightly 6:30PM–10PM
AVERAGE DINNER FOR TWO: $60

CLUB XIX IS classically French, offering award-winning gourmet cuisine.

During the day this irresistible sidewalk bistro serves lunch either indoors or on the outside terrace overlooking the 18th green of Pebble Beach Golf Links. As the evening shadows move across the fairway, the dining mood is elegant, intimate and romantic.

A consistent winner of the Travel Holiday award, Club XIX features the finest fresh fish and produce Monterey has to offer.

The relaxed elegance of The Lodge extends to its 155 spacious guest rooms and six one-bedroom suites. All have either a private patio or balcony offering views of flowering gardens, seaside fairways or spectacular sunsets over Carmel Bay.

The Lodge at Pebble Beach. Since 1919, one of the outstanding resorts of the world.

Poached Pear and Endive Salad
with Roquefort Cheese and Hazelnuts
Abalone in Tarragon Butter Sauce
Crème Brulée

Poached Pear and Endive Salad with Roquefort Cheese and Hazelnuts

Serves 4
Preparation Time: 25 Minutes (note refrigeration time)

1 cup water
1 cup sugar
1 cup red wine
½ orange
½ lemon
½ cinnamon stick
4 pears, peeled, cored, cut into eights
4 cups mixed baby lettuce
¼ cup hazelnuts
4 oz. Roquefort cheese, coarsely crumbled
   Vinaigrette
2 heads Belgian endive

In a large stock pot, combine the water, sugar, red wine, orange, lemon, cinnamon and pears and slowly bring to a simmer. Cook until pears are tender. After pears are poached, allow them to cool.

In a large mixing bowl, combine the baby lettuce, hazelnuts and Roquefort cheese with your favorite vinaigrette.

Divide the salad among four serving plates. Place the pears on top of the lettuce mixture in a circle, with the tips pointing in. Place a piece of endive between each pear.

Abalone in Tarragon Butter Sauce

Serves 4
Preparation Time: 45 Minutes

24 petite abalones
 4 Tbsps. whole butter, room temperature
 1 shallot, chopped fine
⅓ cup tarragon white wine (place one bunch fresh tarragon
 in a bottle of white wine for 48 hours)
 1 cup fish stock
 1 large tomato, peeled, seeded, diced
 1 Tbsp. chopped chives, fresh
 1 Tbsp. chopped tarragon, fresh
 1 lb. saffron angel hair pasta

Place the abalones in a sauté pan with 2 Tbsps. butter and shallots until the butter is melted and the shallots start to cook. Remove the abalones and add the tarragon white wine. Reduce by half.

Add the fish stock and diced tomatoes and reduce the sauce by half again. Finish the sauce with the last 2 Tbsps. of butter, chives and tarragon. Add the abalones and salt and pepper to taste.

Bring boiling salted water to a boil. Add the pasta and cook until al dente, about 1 to 2 minutes. Drain.

To serve, arrange the pasta on the plate with the abalones on top. Ladle the sauce over the abalones.

Crème Brulée

Serves 4
Preparation Time: One Hour (note refrigeration time)
Pre-heat oven to 350°

1 qt. heavy cream
1 vanilla bean, split and scraped
½ cup sugar
12 egg yolks
Raw sugar

Bring the cream and vanilla bean to a simmer over low heat. Steep for 10 to 15 minutes.

In a mixing bowl, beat the sugar and egg yolks until thick and light in color. Slowly add the warmed cream to the yolks, whisking constantly.

Pour mixture into 4 oz. ramekins or custard molds and bake in a shallow water bath covered with foil for 30 to 40 minutes at 350° or until the custard is smooth, glossy and set.

Chill and serve as is for a pot-de-crème or sprinkle the top with 1 heaping teaspoon of raw sugar and caramelize with a salamander or a baker's iron.

CARMEL:
CHIC TO CHIC

YES, VIRGINIA, there was a Carmel before Clint Eastwood came along.

When the actor-director-restaurateur became mayor of the one-square mile village in 1986, his fame drew so many fans that the city council had to move its meetings out of city hall and into a larger facility.

And even today, with Eastwood no longer in office, the most frequent question asked by visitors is a sheepish, "Where's Clint's place?"

Most of the tourists were hoping to catch a glimpse of Eastwood at the Hog's Breath Inn, of which he is a part owner. But Eastwood, who likes his privacy, rarely visited the Hog's Breath. Instead, he bought the Mission Ranch, just outside the city limits, so he could have a place to enjoy dinner in private.

THE LOCATION for Carmel-by-the-Sea was determined in 1771, when Father Junipero Serra moved his mission from Monterey to Carmel. Serra preferred the new location because it offered more fertile land and fresh water.

Using converted Indians as laborers, Serra built the mission and called it Mission San Carlos Borromeo del Rio Carmelo. Still boasting an off-center front window, it is better known as the Carmel Mission Basilica. After his death, Serra was buried at the mission and, in recent years, a growing movement is advocating the declaration of Serra as a saint of the Roman Catholic Church. Pope John Paul II visited the mission in 1987 and blessed Serra's grave.

Clint Eastwood, the former mayor of Carmel.

THE CITY GOT its start in the late 1880s when Santiago Duck-worth, a real estate agent, dreamed of establishing a Catholic resort community to rival the popular Methodist Retreat at Pacific Grove. Working out an agreement with land owner Honore Escolle, Duckworth started selling lots. The first two homes belonged to Davenport Bromfield and Delos Goldsmith (these names are real, honest).

By the turn of the century, the concept of another religious retreat was forgotten. Then along came San Francisco attorney Frank Powers and real estate agent J. Frank Devendorf, who formed the Carmel Development Co., with holdings approximating the present area of the village. These two developers encouraged people of modest means who were interested in the arts. Many a lot was sold for nothing down, pay when you can.

By 1903, the village consisted of 100 people. A population surge occurred in 1885, when David Starr Jordan, president of Stanford University, encouraged professors from Stanford and the University of California to move to Carmel. So many of them moved there that a section near the waterfront came to be called Faculty Row.

ANOTHER SURGE occurred after 1906, when the San Francisco earthquake and fire left homeless a group of artists, musicians and writers. Poet George Sterling and fiery novelist Mary Austin attracted the homeless artists to Carmel. With the Victorian era just ended, the bohemian antics of the free-spirited artists is said to have shocked Carmel residents. Particularly scandalous were the reports of moonlight abalone and mussel feeds, where many jugs of red wine were consumed and barefoot women let loose their long hair as they danced around bonfires in the woods.

THE LONG TRADITION of Carmel as a haven for artists and characters had been born. Their presence set the pattern for the town as a cultural community of free spirits dedicated to preserving their surroundings and the village's unique charm.

The desire to protect the wooded charms of Carmel-by-the-Sea was established with incorporation in 1916. A law dating from that time bans the cutting of trees. Not even a branch of a city-owned tree can be cut unless approved by a commission and permission must be obtained to remove any tree on private property.

A key moment in the preservation of Carmel came with passage of a far-reaching zoning ordinance in 1929. The ordinance dictated that the residential nature of the village should always be more important than business development.

THE ORDINANCE HELPED keep Carmel Beach free of commercial development. The height of buildings was limited, neon and electric signs were prohibited and street lights and sidewalks were discouraged in residential areas.

You may notice that many of the homes in Carmel sport signs with quaint names. That's because Carmel homes have no house numbers. Neither is there any home delivery of mail; residents pick up their mail at the post office and use the occasion to socialize and keep up on the latest gossip.

Another feature that sets Carmel aside are its fairy-tale cottages. Their story began in the 1920s with Mayotta Comstock. Mrs. Comstock made dolls of rags and felt. Her creations were so popular that they drew buyers from all over. The Comstock home was crammed with dolls, so Mayotta convinced her husband, Hugh, to build a large "doll house" in the woods so she could display her dolls. The person-sized house became all the rage and soon merchants wanted doll houses of their own. Perhaps the best known of these is the Tuck Box Tea Room on Ocean Ave.

CARMEL HAS MORE shops than you can shake a credit card at. Scores of shops include upscale boutiques, jewelry shops, antique stores, specialty stores that range from designer toys to handicrafts, art and photography galleries, a large number of chic restaurants and the ever-present Clint Eastwood paraphernalia parlors.

ONE IMPORTANT THING to remember about spending the day in Carmel is that parking space is at a premium. Many parking meters are for short time limits and parking tickets are a large source of income for the village. Car-pooling and parking in garages are recommended.

Special events abound in Carmel. Foremost among the musical events is the prestigious Carmel Bach Festival, founded in 1935. The weeklong programs, staged in July and August, are dedicated to the works of Johann Sebastian Bach, his contemporaries and works of composers influenced by Bach.

Performances are still staged at the Forest Theater, which was founded in 1910 and became city property in 1937. The original stage productions involved most of the townspeople. The Forest Theater was California's first outdoor community theater.

ANOTHER NOTEWORTHY event is the Great Sand Castle Contest, usually held on a Sunday in October at Carmel Beach. Sponsored by a group of architects, the beach blossoms every year with fanciful sand creations and castles, most based on the theme of the year. In order to avoid large crowds, the date of the event and its theme are closely-guarded secrets that are released to the press just a week before the fun-filled event. Bribing of the judges is not only condoned, but actively encouraged.

One last tip: traffic on Highway 1 gets jammed up every afternoon during rush hour, especially in the summer months. Wise visitors plan to stay off Highway 1 just outside Carmel during the commute hours and avoid the Ocean Ave. exit, preferring the Carpenter Street exit.

CARMEL DATEBOOK: Carmel Bach Festival, July and August; Fiesta de San Carlos Borromeo at Carmel Mission Basilica, September; Great Sand Castle Contest, October; Halloween Parade and Carmel Birthday Party, October.

THE COBBLESTONE INN

Junipero between 7th & 8th
P.O. Box 3185
Carmel, CA 93921
(408)625-5222
Rooms $95–$175

THIS COZY INN has a fresh country atmosphere, with a fireplace, telephone, private bath and color television in each of the 24 rooms. Fresh flowers and other amenities will make you feel at home, as will the comfortable sitting area. Quilts, assorted pillows, handsome antiques and fresh fruit are but a few of the guest comforts.

In the morning, a generous breakfast is tastefully prepared and served in the dining room or on the terrace of the courtyard. Each afternoon, tea is served in front of the roaring fire.

The Cobblestone Inn is the perfect retreat for weary travelers, yet it is only one block from the shops and restaurants in Carmel.

Mexican Eggs

Serves 4
Preparation Time: 10 Minutes

  6 eggs
  2 Tbsps. melted butter
 ¼ cup flour
  1 tsp. baking soda
  1 small can green chiles
  2 cups cottage cheese
  2 cups grated cheddar cheese

Whisk together first 4 ingredients and cook over medium heat. Add the chiles and cheeses before stirring.

Double Corn and Cheese Muffins

Preparation Time: 30 Minutes
Pre-heat oven to 400°
Yield: 18 Muffins

1⅓ cups flour
  1 Tbsp. baking powder
  1 tsp. salt
  2 Tbsps. sugar
 ¾ cup cornmeal
  2 eggs
  1 cup milk
 ¼ cup oil
  1 cup creamed corn niblets
 ¼ tsp. rosemary
 ½ green onion, chopped
  2 cups grated cheddar
 ½ cup diced green chiles.

Combine the dry ingredients with the liquid ingredients and add the onions, chiles and cheese. Stir lightly until blended. Bake in greased muffin cups at 400° for 20 minutes.

Basil Chicken Pâté

Preparation Time: One hour
Pre-heat oven to 350°
Yields: 5 mini loaves or one standard loaf

  2 medium yellow onions, chopped
  1 clove garlic, chopped
  2 Tbsps. butter
  4 lbs. raw chicken breasts
    Half of a red pepper
  3 egg whites
2½ cups cream
  1 bunch parsley
  ½ cup packed fresh basil
    Salt and pepper

Sauté the onions and garlic in butter. In a food processor puree the chicken in 2 batches, adding half the cream. Add the onion mixture and egg whites. Process the other half of the chicken, adding the rest of the cream and salt and pepper. Process until chopped. Add ⅓ of the chicken mixture to the parsley and basil. Season with salt and pepper. Process.

Start with the white chicken mixture and spread on the bottom of the bread pan. Next place a few strips of the red pepper on the top. Add the green mixture then the red pepper strips, ending with the white mixture on the top.

Place the pâté pan in another pan filled with water. Cover both pans with foil and bake at 350° for 35-45 minutes.

Spinach and Feta Cheese Triangles

Preparation Time: 45 Minutes (note refrigeration time)
Pre-heat oven to 400°
Yields 35–40

4 Tbsps. oil
3 onions, finely chopped
3 bunches spinach, cooked
2 Tbsps. dill weed
½ lb. feta cheese, crumbled
2 eggs, beaten
6 Tbsps. sour cream
Dash of nutmeg
Salt and pepper
Puff pastry

Sauté the onions in oil until tender. Stir in the spinach and cook over low heat for 5 minutes.

Stir in the dill and cheese. Remove from heat and cool.

Mix in the eggs, sour cream, nutmeg and season with salt and pepper.

Refrigerate until cold.

Cut the puff pastry into 4" squares. Place on a sheet pan with 1 Tbsp. of filling in the center of the pastry. Fold over the opposite corners to form a triangle. Press the edges together with a fork to seal.

Bake at 400° for 15 to 20 minutes.

SAN ANTONIO HOUSE

San Antonio between Ocean & 7th
P.O. Box 2747
Carmel, CA 93921
(408)624-4334
Rooms $100–$130

NESTLED BEHIND AN ivy-covered wall, turn of the century Carmel heritage abounds. Sophisticated and yet casual, amidst the excitement of the Carmel Beach and bustling village, San Antonio House offers romantic seclusion.

Two- and three-room suites are complemented by antiques and a private collection of artwork. Each suite has a private entrance, bath, fireplace and stone patio.

San Antonio House is surrounded by flowering shrubs, expansive tree-shaded lawns, flower-lined walkways and Carmel stone patios and terraces. The gardens are a captivating place to take in the sun and the sound of the sea.

San Antonio House
Carmel By The Sea, Calif.

Buttermilk Bran Muffins

Preparation Time: 15 Minutes
Yields: 2½ dozen muffins

Half of a 15 oz. box raisin bran cereal
2½ cups flour
   2 cups sugar
   1 tsp. salt
   2 tsps. baking soda
   1 tsp. baking powder
   1 tsp. cinnamon
   1 apple, chopped
   2 eggs, beaten
   1 pt. buttermilk
   1 cube margarine
   ½ cup raisins

Mix all the dry ingredients and add the beaten eggs, buttermilk and margarine. Mix well. Add the raisins and apples.
Pour the mixture into greased muffin tins. Bake 25 minutes at 350°.
Remove from the oven and cool. Drizzle the mixed topping over the muffins.

Topping

½ cup flour
½ cup sugar
½ cube margarine
 1 tsp. cinnamon
½ tsp. nutmeg
¼ tsp. ginger

Combine the above ingredients for the muffin topping.

THE SANDPIPER INN

2408 Bay View Ave.
Carmel, CA 93923
(408)624-6433
800-633-6433
Rooms $90–$160

WELCOMING GUESTS WITH warm and gracious hospitality since 1929, the Sandpiper Inn is a romantic bed and breakfast inn, just fifty yards from Carmel Beach.

The inn has 15 individually decorated rooms, furnished with handsome country antiques, fresh flowers and private baths. Many rooms have outstanding ocean views with wood-burning fireplaces.

The comfortable lounge—with cathedral ceilings and Carmel stone fireplace—is the heart of the Inn, where guests enjoy a complimentary continental breakfast and afternoon sherry.

A small, well-stocked library and ten-speed bicycles are available for your enjoyment.

Cranberry Orange Muffins

Preparation Time: 30 Minutes
Pre-heat oven to 375°
Yield: 18 Muffins

2 cups fresh cranberries, chopped
1⅓ cups sugar
6 Tbsps. orange juice
1 Tbsp. orange rind, grated
½ cup butter
1 egg
2 cups flour
1 tsp. baking powder
½ tsp. baking soda
½ tsp. salt

Mix the cranberries with ⅓ cup sugar, orange juice and rind. Set aside.

Cream the butter, adding 1 cup sugar and beaten egg. Add sifted dry ingredients to creamed mixture. Gently mix in cranberries.

Fill greased muffin cups ¾ full. Bake at 375° for 20 minutes.

VAGABOND'S HOUSE INN

4th and Dolores
P.O. Box 2747
Carmel, CA 93921
(408)624-7738
Rooms $79–$135

SITUATED IN THE heart of the village of Carmel, this charming brick half-timbered English Tudor country inn is a delightful experience. It begins as you walk up the front steps to enter an atmosphere that seems almost magical. You'll find yourself in a courtyard dominated by old and very large oak trees, lush with camellias, rhododendrons, hanging plants, ferns and flowers in great profusion.

Accommodations include 11 unique suites, each with a fireplace and private bath. A continental breakfast will be served in your room or in the courtyard each morning.

Vagabond's House is located in the midst of Carmel's finest restaurants, unique shops and well-known art galleries.

Vagabond's House
Carmel·By·The·Sea, California

Chocolate Chip Cheesecake

Serves 10
Preparation Time: 2 Hours (note refrigeration time)
Pre-heat oven to 300°

   2 cups graham cracker crumbs
   ¼ cup sugar
   ½ cup butter, melted
   2 lbs. cream cheese
   1½ cups sugar
   2 Tbsps. flour
   4 eggs, lightly beaten
   ½ tsp. vanilla
   ½ tsp. lemon juice
   1½ cups sour cream
   1 cup chocolate chips

   Mix cracker crumbs with sugar and butter until moist. Press into sides and bottom of 10" springform pan. Refrigerate until needed.

   In a large mixing bowl, beat cream cheese and sugar until smooth, then beat in flour. Add eggs, vanilla and lemon juice, mixing well. Stir in the sour cream and fold in chocolate chips. Pour filling into graham cracker crust.

   Bake for 1½ hours. Turn oven off and leave cheesecake in the oven for another 30 minutes with the oven door ajar. Cool on wire rack.

   Refrigerate overnight before removing from pan.

CASANOVA

MEDITERRANEAN CUISINE
5th between Mission & San Carlos
625-0501
Breakfast Monday–Saturday 8AM–11AM
Lunch 11:30AM–3:00PM
Dinner 5:30PM–10:30PM
Sunday Brunch 9AM–3PM
AVERAGE DINNER FOR TWO: $50

ENTERING CASANOVA'S IS like stepping into the Left Bank of Paris. The inviting interior has touches of Mediterranean blue and muted shades of sienna which are set off by the white washed plaster walls. This charming cafe opens up to a picturesque courtyard, ideal for dining outside.

The menu offers Mediterranean flavors with a contemporary style. The emphasis is on French and Italian cuisine, showing a concern for taste and calories. The healthful, yet satisfying dishes are distinctive in both textures and presentation.

Menu for Four

Smoked Salmon Salad
Pesto Vegetable Soup (Soupe Au Pistou)
Spinach with Cheese (Spinacci Con Olio)
Spaghetti with Beef Tenderloin
(Spaghetti Mimo Di Capri)
Sweet Ricotta Cheese Dessert (Cannoli Alla Siciliana)

Smoked Salmon Salad

Serves 4
Preparation Time: 20 Minutes

½ lb. assorted baby lettuces & herbs, cleaned
   Vinaigrette dressing to taste
2 large tomatoes, sliced
¾ lbs. smoked salmon, sliced
1 red onion, sliced into rings
¼ cup capers
½ lb. goat cheese
2 lemons, sliced

Toss the assorted lettuces and herbs with the vinaigrette. Divide among four plates, surrounded with the sliced tomatoes. Top with smoked salmon, onion rings, capers. Crumble or grate the goat cheese over the salmon.

Decorate with lemon slices.

Pesto Vegetable Soup
(Soupe Au Pistou)

Serves 4
Preparation Time: 2 Hours

3 qts. water
½ cup fava beans, shelled
1 onion, chopped
2 carrots, diced
½ green cabbage, chopped small
2 leeks, chopped, white part only
2 celery stalks, chopped
1 turnip, diced
2 potatoes, diced
¼ lb. cured pork
2 tomatoes, seeded, diced
½ cup snap peas, shelled
½ cup green beans, diced
1 zucchini, diced
4 garlic cloves
10 basil leaves
3 Tsps. olive oil
½ cup Parmesan cheese, grated

Boil water. Add beans, onions, carrots, cabbage, leeks, celery, turnips, potatoes and pork. Simmer for 45 minutes or until beans are tender.

Add tomatoes, snap peas, green beans and zucchini. Simmer for 10 minutes.

In the meantime, make the pistou sauce by crushing the garlic with the basil leaves in a food processor or blender until it makes a paste. Add olive oil at little at a time.

Add the pistou sauce to your soup just before serving. Serve Parmesan to the guests at the table.

Spinach with Cheese (Spinacci Con Olio)

Serves 4
Preparation Time: 15 Minutes

  2 heads spinach, cleaned, stemmed
  1 small head radicchio
    Extra virgin olive oil
  ½ cup Parmesan cheese, grated
  1 lemon, divided into 4 wedges

Steam the spinach. Drain and cool

On four medium salad plates, arrange the radicchio leaves, then the spinach.

Pour the olive oil over all and sprinkle with the Parmesan cheese. Garnish with the lemon wedges.

Spaghetti with Beef Tenderloin (Spaghetti Mimo Di Capri)

Serves 4
Preparation Time: 30 Minutes

3 Tbsps. olive oil
1½ lb. beef tip tenderloin, sliced
1½ cups mushrooms, sliced
2 large tomatoes, diced
1 bunch green onions, chopped
2 cups tomato sauce
3 Tbsps. fresh basil, chopped
1 lb. spaghetti
1 cup Parmesan cheese, grated

In a sauté pan, heat the olive oil and add the beef tips. Sear them very quickly over high heat. Add the mushrooms, tomatoes, green onions and sauté together for 2 minutes. Add the tomato sauce and simmer until sauce is warm. Add the chopped basil.

Meanwhile, cook spaghetti in a large pot of boiling salted water until al dente, drain and cool with cold water.

Divide spaghetti among 4 large plates. With a ladle, dish out your sauce on the spaghetti. Sprinkle with Parmesan cheese and serve.

Sweet Ricotta Cheese Dessert (Cannoli Alla Siciliana)

Serves 4
Preparation Time: 1½ Hours

  1 cup flour
  1 egg
  1 Tbsp. sugar
  1 Tbsp. butter
  ¼ cup Marsala wine
    Pinch of salt
    Pinch of cinnamon
    Cannoli tubes (special equipment)
  1 lb. whole milk ricotta cheese
  ½ cup powdered sugar
    Grated rind of half lemon
  ¼ cup semisweet chocolate, chopped
    Pistachio nuts, chopped

Make a well in the flour and add the egg, sugar, butter, Marsala wine, salt and cinnamon. Knead 10 minutes. Cover and rest for 1 hour.

Roll the dough flat into a square. Place square on cannoli tubes and fry until golden brown.

Prepare the filling by mixing together the ricotta cheese, powdered sugar, lemon rind and chocolate. Refrigerate.

Fill shells just before serving and decorate with pistachios.

CREME CARMEL

FRENCH CUISINE
San Carlos and 7th Street
Carmel
624-0444
Dinner nightly 5:30PM–10PM
AVERAGE DINNER FOR TWO: $50

Excellent seasonal cuisine sums up the philosophy of Creme Carmel. Using only the finest ingredients available to inspire many creative and tasteful dishes.

Dining at Creme Carmel will delight the most discriminating palate as well as the most ardent romantic. The setting is Country French; simple, charming yet elegant. White table linens and china are the backdrop for the extraordinary cuisine.

The service is first class and unpretentious. The wine list is well chosen. Reservations are recommended.

Menu for Six

Maine Lobster Soup
with Water Chestnuts and Baby Corn
Lamb Loin with Rosemary and Garlic
Apple Mint Chutney
Chocolate Soufflé

Maine Lobster Soup with Water Chestnuts and Baby Corn

Serves 6
Preparation Time: 1½ Hours

Two 1 lb. lobsters
1 onion
2 carrots
3 celery ribs
1 bay leaf
12 peppercorns
¼ lemon
1 tsp. thyme
6 cloves
1 Tbsp. paprika
1 cup sherry

Pinch cayenne pepper
6 fresh water chestnuts,
    peeled and chopped
6 ears baby corn, or 2 ears
    fresh sweet corn shaved
    from cob
Salt and white pepper to
    taste

Chop the vegetables and cover with enough water to also cover lobsters. Bring the water to a boil. Put the lobsters in boiling water for 3 minutes. Remove the pot from the stove and let stand for 15 minutes. Remove lobsters. When cool, remove meat from the tail and claws and refrigerate. Put the shells back into the water and boil for 45 minutes. Strain out and reserve all the liquid. Add sherry and seasonings, then reduce liquid to about 2 qts.

Five minutes before serving, add the chestnuts and corn. Two minutes before serving, add the chopped lobster.

For a richer, creamy lobster soup, thicken with roux and add some cream or half and half.

Lamb Loin with Rosemary and Garlic

Serves 6
Preparation Time: 20 Minutes (note cooking time)
Pre-heat oven to 400°

3 boned lamb loins
(approximately 2 lbs.)
2 Tbsps. butter
2 Tbsps. flour
1 cup white wine
3 cups lamb/veal stock

2 Tbsps. rosemary, finely
chopped
4 cloves garlic, pressed
½ tomato, peeled, seeded
and diced

Make the sauce first by making roux with butter and flour. Cook over low heat until nutty brown. Add the wine, stock, rosemary, garlic and tomatoes. Boil gently until reduced by ⅓.

Lightly oil a large skillet and sear lamb for 10 seconds on all sides. Place the lamb on a rack with a pan under the rack, in the oven. Place the rosemary and garlic on each loin. Bake at 400° to desired doneness (8 minutes for medium rare).

Slice and add sauce.

Apple-Mint Chutney

Preparation Time: 25 Minutes

4 Granny Smith apples,
chopped
½ cup onion, finely chopped
2 garlic cloves, pressed
3 Tbsps. fresh mint,
chopped

1½ tsps. dried tarragon
⅛ tsp. white pepper
A pinch of nutmeg
1 cup white wine vinegar
⅓ cup white wine
⅓ cup sugar

Combine all the ingredients except the sugar and cook in a large skillet over medium high heat until most of the liquid is gone. Add the sugar. Cook and stir 3 more minutes.

Cool and refrigerate.

Chocolate Soufflé

Serves 6
Preparation Time: 35 Minutes
Pre-heat oven to 375°

6 Tbsps. butter
½ cup flour
½ cup milk
⅓ cup cream
7 oz. bittersweet chocolate
⅔ cup sugar
   Whiskey and cognac to equal ⅓ cup
6 eggs, separated

Cook the butter and flour gently for 5 minutes. Add the milk and cream all at once. Cook over medium heat, stirring frequently for 10 minutes.

While cooking the milk, melt the chocolate in a mixing bowl over hot water. When the milk is very thick and sticky add whiskey, cognac and sugar. Cook 3 more minutes.

Separate the eggs, putting the yolks into a mixing bowl. While stirring the chocolate, add the milk mixture. When completely mixed, stir yolks and add the chocolate mixture.

Whip the egg whites with a pinch of salt until stiff. Fold into the chocolate mixture.

Bake at 375° for 15 minutes in individual dishes.

PACIFIC'S EDGE RESTAURANT

CALIFORNIA CUISINE
Highlands Inn
P.O. Box 1700
Carmel, CA 93921
624-3801
Lunch daily 11:30AM–2PM
Dinner nightly 6PM–10PM
AVERAGE DINNER FOR TWO: $70

PACIFIC'S EDGE RESTAURANT, located in the Highlands Inn at the edge of Big Sur and minutes from Carmel, offers spectacular ocean and coastal views. You will dine in an open and inviting room where you can watch the rolling Pacific swells surge toward shore. Every evening provides a dramatic sunset, giving way to a million stars.

The Executive Chef specializes in presenting the freshest and finest California cuisines, carefully prepared with Salinas Valley produce, California meats and poultry and Monterey Bay seafood.

Laced throughout the inn's wooded acres are flowering walkways, hidden hot tubs and scores of cottages and townhouses. Each accommodation includes a wood-burning fireplace and vista deck.

The townhouse units offer a custom-furnished parlor, full kitchen, master bedroom and bath with a massive spa tub.

Visit soon!

HIGHLANDS INN

Rosemary Vinaigrette

Yield: 1 cup
Preparation Time: 5 Minutes

¾ **cup extra virgin olive oil**
⅓ **cup balsamic vinegar or sherry wine vinegar**
1 **tsp. chopped rosemary**
   Salt and freshly ground pepper to taste

Place all the ingredients in a small bowl. Hold a wire whisk upright in the bowl, and rotate it between the palms of your hands until the vinaigrette is well blended.

Sardine Filets on Potatoes

Serves 4
Preparation Time: 45 Minutes (note refrigeration time)

6 fresh sardines
Salt and pepper to taste
1 cup olive oil
1 onion, sliced
1 bunch thyme
2 large baking potatoes, diced

1 bunch basil, chopped
1 tsp. balsamic vinegar
1 bunch chives, chopped fine
2 shallots, chopped fine
10 black olives, oil cured, chopped
2 tomatoes, diced

Filet the sardines with a sharp knife by cutting off the head and running the knife down both sides of the backbone (or ask the fish monger to filet and clean the fish for you). What you should have is 12 filets of semi-boneless fish.

Place the sardines on a sheet pan, skin side down and lightly season with salt and pepper.

In a sauté pan, heat 2 Tbsps. olive oil over medium heat. Place the filets skin side up and cook for 2 minutes or until fish is cooked through. Don't turn the fish skin side down. The sardine skin is a beautiful blue-silver and when you cook the sardine on the skin it generally shrinks and tears.

Place sliced onions on a clean sheet pan and top with thyme.

With a spatula, carefully remove the cooked filet and place on top of the onions, skin side up. Allow the filets to cool in the refrigerator, then pour ½ cup olive oil over the filets before covering them with wax paper or foil. The filets will keep up to 7 days in the refrigerator.

Cook the potatoes in salted water until soft. Remove from heat and purée with ¼ cup olive oil in a blender. When potatoes have cooled, add the basil, shallots and balsamic vinegar.

Place the potato mixture into a pastry bag and pipe out the basil potatoes the length of each sardine filet, skin side down.

To serve, lay the sardine filet skin side up on top of the potatoes. Discard the onion and thyme. Sprinkle the filets with black olives, chives and tomatoes. Drizzle with rosemary vinaigrette.

Roasted Beef Tenderloin with Chanterelles and Braised Leeks

Serves 4
Preparation Time: 45 Minutes (note marinating time)
Pre-heat oven to 350°

      2 lbs. beef tenderloin
      4 large garlic cloves, peeled, crushed
      1 bunch thyme
 1¼ cups olive oil
      3 lbs. chanterelles
      3 garlic cloves, chopped
         Salt and pepper to taste
      2 large leeks
      1 cup chicken stock

Trim the tenderloin of all silverskin (outer white membrane). Marinate the meat in the garlic, thyme and 1 cup olive oil overnight in the refrigerator.

Cut chanterelles in large chunks to maintain the natural shape of the mushroom. Sauté over high heat in 2 Tbsps. olive oil until the liquid is cooked out and the mushrooms are becoming caramelized. At that point, add the chopped garlic and salt and pepper to taste, being careful not to burn the garlic. Reserve and set aside.

Cut the leeks crosswise, just below the green leaves. Take the white of the leek and slice lengthwise in half. Wash in cold water, cut crosswise into ¼" half rings. Place in a pan with the chicken stock, salt and pepper and cook over medium heat until the liquid is gone and the leeks are soft. You may add 1 Tbsp. butter, if desired. Set aside.

Remove the beef from the marinade and season well with salt and pepper. Heat 2 Tbsps. olive oil in a sauté pan and sear the beef until it is golden brown on all sides. Remove from the pan and roast in a 350° oven for 15–20 minutes. Let rest in a warm place for 10 minutes before serving.

As the meat is resting, reheat the leeks and mushrooms.

A nice variation is to add a little veal stock to the mushrooms for a sauce or make a ragout of mushrooms and leeks when rewarming. You may also choose to grill the meat instead of roasting.

Roasted Rack of Lamb

Serves 4
Preparation Time: 30 Minutes (note marinating time)

2 racks of lamb
1 cup olive oil
4 large cloves garlic, crushed
1 bunch rosemary
  Salt and pepper to taste

Trim lamb of excess fat or ask the butcher to do it.

Combine the olive oil, garlic, rosemary, salt and pepper in a small bowl, and mix well. Place the lamb in a nonreactive baking pan. Pour the mixture over the lamb, cover, and refrigerate overnight or longer, turning the lamb frequently.

Prepare the hot coals for grilling. Remove the lamb from the marinade and season well with salt and pepper. Place on a hot grill. When the lamb is well seared, move to a cooler part of the grill and cook slowly for approximately 15 minutes or to desired doneness.

The following recipe of the stuffed tomatoes with potato risotto is a wonderful accompaniment to the rack of lamb.

Tomatoes
Stuffed with Potato Risotto

Serves 4
Preparation Time: 1½ Hours

  6 tomatoes
  2 large potatoes
  1 cup cream
  2 garlic cloves, chopped
  1 rosemary sprig, chopped
  1 cup chicken stock
  ⅓ cup goat cheese
  ⅓ cup Parmesan cheese
     Extra virgin olive oil

Blanch the tomatoes in salted boiling water for 30 seconds, just to remove the skins. Place in an ice water bath.

When tomatoes are cool, remove all outer skin and cut off ½" of the top, reserving the tops for later use. Remove the inside of the tomato to form a cup.

Peel and slice the potatoes in ⅟16" cubes. Place in a small pan over low heat and cook with the cream, chopped garlic and chopped rosemary until thick. Add the chicken stock, goat cheese and Parmesan cheese. Stir over low heat for about 45 minutes or until the potatoes are al dente.

Stuff the tomatoes with the potato risotto mixture and cover with the tomato tops.

Heat the tomatoes in 500° oven until warmed. Drizzle with extra virgin olive oil before serving.

PIATTI RISTORANTE

ITALIAN CUISINE
Corner of Junipero & 6th Ave.
Carmel
625-1766
Monday–Friday lunch 11:30AM–2:30PM
Dinner 5PM–10PM
Saturday–Sunday Noon–10PM
AVERAGE DINNER FOR TWO: $35

SINCE ITS FOUNDING in 1987, Ristorante Piatti has become one of the food industry's shining success stories. From one restaurant, Piatti has grown to six restaurants—with more on the way. The casual atmosphere and traditional regional Italian cuisine draw diners from every point of the globe.

The open kitchen, wood-burning oven, red-tiled floor, big windows and white pine furnishings provide the right ambiance for the innovative menu. Piatti is an authentic Italian restaurant, as friendly and inviting as a neighborhood trattoria.

Bon appetit.

RISTORANTE PIATTI

Menu for Four

Gorgonzola Salad
Fettuccine with Chicken and Mushrooms
Tiramisu with Crème Anglaise

Gorgonzola Salad

Serves 4
Preparation Time: 10 Minutes

8 whole Belgian endives
2 Tbsps. lemon juice
1 Tbsp. Italian parsley, chopped
⅓ cup extra virgin olive oil
1 Tbsp. walnut oil
   Salt and fresh ground pepper
1 cup walnuts, toasted
8 oz. gorgonzola, cut into 8 thin slices

Separate endive spears into a large bowl. Set aside.

In a small mixing bowl, whisk together the lemon juice, parsley, oils, salt and pepper to taste. Pour over the endive and add the walnuts. Toss gently to avoid bruising the endive.

Divide among 4 chilled salad plates. Top each salad with 2 slices of gorgonzola.

Fettuccine with Chicken and Mushrooms

Serves 4
Preparation Time: 30 Minutes

1 **head fennel, julienned**
2 **Tbsps. olive oil**
2 **cups crimini or button mushrooms, sliced**
1 **Tbsp. fresh thyme**
2 **cups roast chicken, diced**
½ **cup dry sherry**
1 **lb. fresh fettuccine pasta**
1 **cup chicken stock**
2 **Tbsps. butter**
1 **Tbsp. Italian parsley, chopped**
  Parmesan cheese, optional

Bring a large pot of salted water to a boil.

Sauté the fennel in olive oil over low heat until soft and beginning to brown. Add the mushrooms and sauté until the mushrooms begin to brown. Add the thyme and chicken. When the chicken is warmed through, add the sherry, allow the sherry to reduce by half.

Add the pasta to the hot water and cook 3–5 minutes or until the pasta is al dente.

While the pasta is cooking, add the chicken stock to the chicken-mushroom mixture. When it boils, add the butter and parsley.

Drain the pasta well but do not rinse. Add the pasta to the chicken mixture. Toss to distribute pasta and divide among 4 warm plates.

Serve with freshly grated Parmesan cheese.

Tiramisu

Serves 4
Preparation Time: 30 Minutes (note refrigeration time)

 3 egg yolks
 1 cup mascarpone cheese
 ¼ cup sugar
 ½ cup cream, whipped
 1 box lady fingers (about 50 pieces)
 7 cups espresso or strong coffee
 ½ cup dark rum
   Ground chocolate

In a mixer, beat eggs, mascarpone and sugar until fluffy and creamy. Fold in whipped cream. Set aside.

Combine the coffee and rum. Dip each lady finger in the coffee rum mixture, sugar side down, for 1 second. Lady fingers get soggy very quickly.

Layer lady fingers in a 3″ deep rectangular pan. Cover with mascarpone mixture. Repeat procedure until all the mascarpone and lady fingers are used. Chill for 2 hours.

Garnish with ground chocolate and crème anglaise.

Crème Anglaise

 7 egg yolks
 ½ cup sugar
 2 cups milk
 2 tsps. vanilla extract

In a mixing bowl, whisk together the egg yolks and sugar for about 2 minutes. Set aside.

In a double boiler, over medium heat, bring milk and vanilla to a boil. Add the egg mixture to the milk and whisk quickly so eggs don't curdle. Cook until 145° is reached. Cool before serving.

RAFFAELLO RESTAURANT

ITALIAN CUISINE
Mission between Ocean and 7th Ave.
Carmel
624-1541
Dinner nightly 6PM-10PM
Closed Tuesday
AVERAGE DINNER FOR TWO: $40

THIS INTIMATE AND elegant Northern Italian ristorante offers a true adventure in hospitality. Owner-chef Remo d'Agliano is dedicated to providing a dining experience second to none.

As you enter Raffaello's, you will be treated to the aroma of fresh garlic and herbs. The menu is innovative and intriguing, offering classic regional delicacies.

An evening at Raffaello Restaurant is a blend of impeccable service, superb cuisine and great wine.

Menu for Four

Fettuccine al Doppio Burro
Veal with Mushrooms
Chocolate Soufflé

Fettuccine al Doppio Burro

Serves 4
Pre-heat oven to 350°
Preparation Time: 15 Minutes

1 lb. egg noodles
½ cup sweet butter
½ cup plus 2 Tbsps. Parmesan cheese, grated
¼ cup heavy cream

Boil the noodles in salted water until al dente. Drain well.

Melt the butter and ½ cup Parmesan cheese on low heat and pour over the cooked noodles. Add the cream and toss well.

Pour the noodle mixture into a buttered baking dish. Sprinkle the top with 2 Tbsps. of Parmesan cheese and bake at 350° for 10 minutes.

Serve hot and bubbly.

Veal with Mushrooms

Serves 4
Preparation Time: 45 Minutes

4 veal chops
1 medium onion, sliced into rounds
3 Tbsps. olive oil
2 Tbsps. butter
½ cup flour
   Salt and pepper to taste
½ cup dry white wine
1 lemon, sliced into rings
5 tomatoes, peeled and chopped
1 oz. dried Porcini mushrooms

Sauté the onions in a large frying pan, using the olive oil and butter, until they are limp.

Flour the veal chops and add to the onions. Brown them well on both sides, adding salt and pepper to taste. Add the wine and lemon rings. When the wine has evaporated, remove the veal chops. Add the tomatoes and mushrooms to the sauce and cook on moderate heat for 15 minutes.

Put the veal chops back into the frying pan, cover and heat through until warm.

Serve immediately.

A suggested vegetable to accompany this meal is spinach, sautéed in butter or olive oil and garlic.

Chocolate Soufflé

Serves 4
Preparation Time: 20 Minutes
Pre-heat oven to 350°
Yields: 6 inch soufflé dish

3 oz. chocolate
¼ cup plus 1½ Tbsps. granulated sugar
3 Tbsps. milk
2 egg yolks
3 egg whites
¾ cup chocolate sauce
   Garnish with whipped cream or chocolate sauce

In a double-boiler, melt the chocolate, sugar and the milk, beating until well mixed. Remove from the heat and allow it to cool for a few minutes. Add the egg yolks, beating constantly. Set aside.

Whip the egg whites until they are very stiff, adding 1½ Tbsps. sugar halfway through. Fold the egg whites into the chocolate mixture.

Pour into a buttered and sugared soufflé mold. Bake 20 minutes at 350°.

Serve the soufflé with whipped cream or cool chocolate sauce.

RIO GRILL

CALIFORNIA CUISINE
101 Crossroads Blvd.
Carmel, CA 93923
625-5436
Lunch daily 11:30AM–4PM
Dinner nightly 5PM–10PM
AVERAGE DINNER FOR TWO: $35

CREATIVE AMERICAN FOOD is well represented at the Rio Grill, where the freshest ingredients and oakwood smoker give the innovative appetizers and exciting entrees a wonderful flair.

What is there to eat? Start with the warm goat cheese, coated with almonds and nestled in a bed of endive and watercress, smothered with sun dried tomatoes, or the rabbit quesadilla with ancho chile and roasted tomatillo salsa. For the adventurous, how about a whole head of roasted garlic that has been bathed in olive oil and browned on the grill. Slice off the top and spread this outrageous mixture on sourdough bread. Exquisite! Fresh fish, herbed chicken, mustard-glazed duck and barbecued ribs pass through The Rio Grill's oak-burning oven-smoker.

The comfortable "Santa Fe" setting provides the perfect background for an intimate dinner or cocktails.

Roasted Garlic
Corn Salad with Steamed and Dressed Asparagus
Grilled Rabbit with Mustard Greens, Ginger and Sage

Roasted Garlic

Serves 4
Preparation Time: 5 Minutes (note cooking time)
Pre-heat oven to 375°

1 large head of garlic
1 Tbsp. olive oil
Sliced sourdough bread or toast points

Cut the top off the garlic and place root side down in a roasting pan. Sprinkle with olive oil and cover. Roast at 375° until soft. Approximately 60-90 minutes.

Slice the top off, so that the melted cloves can be scooped out and spread on sourdough bread or toast points.

Corn Salad with Steamed and Dressed Asparagus

Serves 4
Preparation Time: 15 Minutes

½ lb. asparagus
½ cup rice vinegar
1 cup olive oil
1 Tbsp. mint, chopped
1 Tbsp. basil, chopped
  Salt and pepper to taste
2 cups shucked sweet corn
1 peeled avocado, sliced
1 green onion, minced

Blanch the asparagus in hot water for 5 minutes or until tender when pricked with a fork. Let cool.

Combine ¼ cup rice vinegar and ¼ cup olive oil and coat the asparagus. Set aside.

Mix the remaining vinegar, olive oil and herbs together. Season with salt and pepper. Mix in the corn, avocado and onion.

On a large platter, lay a strip of the corn salad at an angle across from the asparagus diagonally. Alternate with strips of corn salad and asparagus.

Grilled Rabbit with Mustard Greens, Ginger and Sage

Serves 6
Preparation Time: 45 Minutes (note marinating time)

 2 rabbits
¼ cup olive oil
¼ bunch thyme, chopped
 1 tsp. white pepper
¼ cup Dijon mustard
 1 cup white wine
⅓ cup lemon juice
¼ bunch sage
 1 inch peeled ginger, coarsely chopped
 2 shallots, chopped
 2 Tbsps. cream
 1 lb. salted butter
 1 red onion, sliced
 4 shiitake mushrooms, sliced
 3 cups mustard greens, cut 1 inch wide

Cut rabbits into 6 pieces. Front legs, back legs with thigh bone removed and boneless loin sections (saddles).

Combine olive oil, thyme, pepper and mustard. Marinate the rabbits for at least six hours.

Grill the front legs first (they take the longest), then back legs and saddle.

In a stainless saucepan over medium heat, combine white wine, lemon juice, sage, ginger and shallots for the sauce. Reduce all of these ingredients until dry. Add the cream and reduce by half. Build up with butter, a little at a time, whisking constantly over medium heat. Strain and add sage and ginger.

Just before serving, mix the onion, mushrooms and mustard greens. Place the rabbit over the greens and cover with the sauce.

ROBATA GRILL AND SAKE BAR

JAPANESE CUISINE
3658 The Barnyard
Carmel, CA 93921
624-2643
Dinner nightly 5PM–10PM
AVERAGE DINNER FOR TWO: $35

EXPERIENCE "OPEN HEARTH" cooking at this outstanding Japanese restaurant.

The menu offers an extensive list of appetizers from which you can put together a delicious dinner, as well as fresh mesquite grilled fish and unique dinner combinations.

The atmosphere is fun and authentic. The service is excellent.

The Robata Grill and Sake Bar is a delightful restaurant to savor a fine meal or enjoy a few drinks, in a distinctive setting.

grill and sake bar

Menu for Four

Nikumaki (Filet Mignon Roll)
Shiitake Salmon
Yasai (Veggies) with Sesame Cream
Onigiri (BBQ Rice Ball)

Nikumaki

Serves 4
Preparation Time: 45 Minutes

12 oz. thinly sliced filet mignon (sliced by butcher)
4 stalks of green onions
½ cup soy sauce
½ cup sugar
4 slices fresh ginger
3 oz. sake
Orange slice for garnish

Combine soy sauce, sugar, ginger and sake in a heavy saucepan, over low heat until sugar is dissolved and ginger shrivels. Set aside.

Divide thin slices of filet mignon into four equal 3-oz. portions. Lay out the filets so each portion equals a 4"x6" rectangle.

Take one stalk of green onion and fold in half. Place on lower half of filet rectangle, then roll up to form sausage-like tube of filet with green onion in the center.

While forming Nikumaki, have your barbecue hot and ready for cooking. Cook to desired doneness. Remove from the fire and cut into one inch portions. Arrange on a small platter with a slice of orange, then dribble sauce over the Nikumaki and serve.

Vegies with Sesame Cream

Serves 4
Preparation Time: 15 Minutes

2 large carrots
2 green zucchinis
2 daikon
¼ lb. string beans
2 eggs
1 cup vegetable oil
1 Tbsp. sesame oil
¼ cup soy sauce
2 garlic cloves, pressed
1 Tbsp. rice vinegar

Julienne all the vegetables to 3 inch long matchsticks.

Bring salted water to a boil and put the vegetables in the water for 1 minute and remove.

In a mixing bowl, with two egg yolks whisk the vegetable oil in very slowly, to emulsify. When the consistency is like mayonnaise, add the remaining ingredients and blend together.

Spoon on vegetables.

Barbecued Rice Balls (Onigiri)

2 cups short grain rice
Sauce from Nikumaki

Wash the rice and put it in a heavy pot. Cover with water ¾ inches above the level of the rice. Bring to a boil over high heat. Cover and reduce the heat to cook for 20 minutes. Let the rice cool after cooking.

Wet hands and form rice into thick hamburger patty. Brush with Nikumaki Sauce and grill on the barbecue until marked. Serve immediately.

Shiitake Salmon

4 salmon fillets, 8 oz. each
½ cup vegetable oil
1 cup shiitake mushrooms, sliced
1 Tbsp. garlic, minced
1 Tbsp. ginger, minced
2 Tbsps. soy sauce
Salt to taste
1 stalk green onion, chopped

Rub the salmon fillets with the vegetable oil and lightly salt. Place on barbecue.

Heat ¼ cup oil in a sauté pan over high heat, until light smoke appears. Add the mushrooms, garlic and ginger to cook for 20 seconds. Remove the pan from the heat and add the soy sauce.

Remove the grilled salmon from the barbecue. Top the salmon with the shiitake mushrooms and decorate with chopped green onions.

Fill the plates with fresh blanched vegetables and onigiri.

SANS SOUCI

FRENCH CUISINE
Lincoln between 5th & 6th Street
Carmel
624-6220
Dinner nightly from 6PM
Closed Wednesdays
AVERAGE DINNER FOR TWO: $40

EXQUISITE CLASSIC FRENCH cuisine, a flickering fireplace, sparkling crystal chandeliers and brilliantly colored flower bouquets best describe Sans Souci—"without worry"—truly apropos. Owned and operated by John Williams, Sans Souci has been in the family for 18 years, and its tradition for excellence is world renowned.

The menu combines classical with contemporary French cuisine. The emphasis is to use natural ingredients, the freshest herbs, with little or no cream, but still offer those wonderful dishes rich in tradition. Selections include entrees such as Sautéed Maine Lobster in a Broth of Oyster Mushrooms, Tomatoes and fresh Herbs, Filet mignon with Shallots, Onions and Black Truffles and Abalone with an Orange Sabayon Sauce.

One of the most romantic restaurants on the Peninsula.

Sans
Souci

RESTAURANT
Since 1971

Menu for Four

Goat Cheese Fritters, Apricot Sauce
Salmon with Grapefruit Butter
Chocolate Cake

Goat Cheese Fritters, Apricot Sauce

Serves 4
Preparation Time: 15 Minutes

  2 cups flour
  1 egg
    Pinch of sugar
 12 oz. beer
 20 dried apricots
  2 cups dark red port
  1 lb. goat cheese
    Salt and white pepper to taste
  2 cups peanut oil
  1 bunch of watercress

In a mixing bowl combine the flour, egg, pinch of sugar and all but a sip of the beer. Mix well and let rest for ½ hour.

In a sauce pot place dried apricots and cover them with port, cooking over a low flame until apricots become soft and only half of the liquid surrounds them.

Form the goat cheese into 8 equal size balls and season them with salt and white pepper.

Begin to heat oil until it reaches 350° or until it is hot enough to fry quickly a test droplet of batter. Drop the goat cheese balls one at a time, first into batter then into hot oil. Cook approximately 1 minute or until they are crispy and golden brown.

On a warm platter pour apricots and their port syrup. Arrange the fritters on top and garnish with sprigs of fresh watercress.

Salmon with Grapefruit Butter

Serves 4
Preparation Time: 30 Minutes

  2 lbs. salmon filets (cut into 4 portions)
  8 ruby red grapefruits, peeled, quartered
  ½ cup sugar
  2 Tbsps. unsalted butter, cubed
  ½ tsp. pink peppercorns
  8 chives

Season the salmon filets and poach them 5 minutes over a low flame.

Combine 24 grapefruit quarters and sugar in a sauce pot over medium heat until the juice has the consistency of a thick syrup. Add the butter, cube by cube, until it is completely incorporated into the juice. Season with salt and pepper.

Remove the salmon filets from the stock, being sure to drain all excess liquid before placing them on a warm platter.

Pour the sauce over the salmon and garnish with the remaining 8 grapefruit sections, pink peppercorns and chives.

Chocolate Cake

Preparation Time: 30 Minutes
Pre-heat oven to 350°

8 eggs, separated
1 cup sugar
1 cup cake flour, sifted
4 Tbsps. (½ stick) unsalted butter, melted
3 oz. dark French style chocolate

Whip the egg whites to firm peaks and set aside, keeping them cold. Mix the yolks and sugar in a electric blender for 5 minutes or until yolks "ribbon." Slowly add all the flour, melted butter and melted chocolate. Fold in the egg whites.

Pour into a floured 10″ cake pan and bake for 10–15 minutes at 350? The cake is done when a toothpick comes out dry after being inserted in the middle of the cake. Cool on a rack.

Frosting

½ lb. chocolate
3 eggs, separated
¼ lb. unsalted butter, cubed
⅛ cup hot cream
   Whipped cream, garnish
   Fresh fruit, garnish

Add the melted chocolate to the egg yolks and blend in the hot cream. Slowly add the butter cubes one at a time until completely blended.

Whip egg whites until firm and fold into the chocolate mixture.

Pour the frosting over the cooled cake. Chill both and serve with whipped cream and fresh fruit garnish.

SILVER JONES RESTAURANT

CALIFORNIA CUISINE
The Barnyard
Carmel
624-5200
Lunch and dinner daily
11:30AM–3PM, 5:30PM–9:30PM
AVERAGE DINNER FOR TWO: $35

IF YOU WANT fresh, local, pristine ingredients, an imaginative touch in the kitchen, and a healthy, hearty serving at a fair price, look no further. At Silver Jones, you will find a warm, firelit greeting in the oak-floored dining room. Afghan carpets and strings of fresh chiles complete the casual, elegant, but slightly irreverent ambience.

Owners Jack Silver and Michael Jones are always around to see to details, and chef Tom Vitale's crew is as speedy as it is skillful.

The large selection of fresh fish and pastas, organic salads, and outrageous desserts is exquisite.

Pico de Gallo
(Apple, Jicama, Shrimp, Scallops)

Serves 6
Preparation Time: 20 Minutes (note marinating time)

½ lb. shrimp or small prawns
½ lb. scallops
2 Granny Smith apples
1 medium jicama
3 limes
1 tsp. cumin

1 tsp. coriander
½ tsp. cayenne
Tomato salsa garnish
Guacamole or chopped
avocado garnish

Blanch the shrimp in a large pot of boiling water. Peel if necessary, set aside and chill.

Blanch the scallops for 30 seconds. Reserve and chill.

Core and peel the apples and cut into medium-small pieces. Peel the jicama and cut into the same shapes.

In a large bowl, combine the jicama, apples and shellfish. Squeeze the juice of the limes and toss. Sprinkle in the cumin, coriander and cayenne and gently toss.

Let marinate for several hours.

Spoon into compote dishes and garnish with avocado and fresh salsa.

Cooking tip: Serve with freshly fried flour tortilla wedges.

Roasted Sweet Pepper and Tomato Soup

Serves 6
Preparation Time: 20 Minutes (note refrigeration time)

    3 red bell peppers
    1 fresh ancho (pasilla) chile
   10 Roma tomatoes
      Half a cucumber
    1 cup garlic cloves, whole
   ½ cup olive oil
   ¼ cups white vinegar
      Creme fraiche or sour cream garnish

Roast the bell and ancho peppers under a very hot broiler until the skin blackens. Put peppers in a small bowl and cover.

Peel the tomatoes by dropping in boiling water for 20 seconds. Remove them and quickly plunge them in cold water. Cut in half and gently press out the seeds.

Peel the cucumber, cut in half and strip out the seeds with the back of a teaspoon.

Poach the garlic cloves in the olive oil until they are soft and white (slowly!). By now the peppers are cooled, so peel them under running water and strip out the seeds.

Throw everything in the blender and let it rip. Chill thoroughly. Garnish with creme fraiche or sour cream.

Cooking tip: Depending on the size and moisture content of the vegetables, the consistency may vary. You may want to have a 6 oz. can of V-8 juice to keep the blender flowing smoothly.

Wild Rice & Three Mushroom Salad with Baby Spinach

Serves 6
Preparation Time: 45 Minutes

2 ½ cups water
1 cup wild rice
½ onion, chopped
4 cloves garlic, chopped
2 bay leaves
½ cup olive oil
¼ cup walnut pieces
¼ cup pine nuts
2 cups mushrooms, Shiitake, Cremini or white
1 bunch parsley, finely chopped
1 bunch green onions, finely chopped
¼ cup white vinegar
2 cups spinach, cleaned
Juice of 1 lemon
Roasted eggplant garnish

Bring water to a boil in a large pot. Add the rice, onion, garlic and bay leaves and simmer until cooked. Remove from heat and cool.

Heat the olive oil in a sauce pan. Add the walnuts and pine nuts, stirring constantly. Remove from heat when the pine nuts are a light brown. Cool.

Coarsely chop the mushrooms and toss into the cooked rice mixture. Add the parsley, green onion, vinegar and the browned nuts.

In a separate bowl, toss the spinach with the lemon juice. Place the spinach in the middle of a serving platter and ring the wild rice salad around the spinach.

Garnish with roasted eggplant.

Penne Pasta Pancetta

Serves 6
Preparation Time: 20 Minutes

3 Tbsps. olive oil
½ lb. pancetta, coarsely chopped
¼ cup pine nuts
½ large eggplant, coarsely chopped
4 cloves garlic, finely chopped
½ onion, coarsely chopped
1 leek, finely chopped
¼ cup Calamata olives, hulled, chopped
¼ cup sun-dried tomatoes, chopped
   Dried herbs: mix fennel seed, oregano, basil, lavender flowers
   (the secret ingredient!), black pepper
   Penne Rigate pasta, cooked
½ cup chicken stock
4 Roma tomatoes, coarsely chopped

This is a sauté. Heat olive oil in a large, heavy-bottomed sauce pan. Add the pancetta and toss until lightly browned.

Add the pine nuts and toss until lightly browned. Add the eggplant, stirring until cooked through. Add the garlic and onion and cook lightly.

Add the leeks, olives and sun-dried tomatoes with several good pinches of dried herbs. Add the cooked pasta and gently stir everything together. Add a little chicken stock to moisten the mix if necessary.

Just before serving, add the fresh tomatoes.

Bread Pudding

Serves 6
Preparation Time: 30 Minutes
Pre-heat oven to 375°

  2 soft bananas
  ½ cup brown sugar
  2 eggs
  ½ cup milk
  4 Tbsps. soft butter
  ½ cup raisins, soaked in whiskey
  1 Tbsp. allspice
  1 tsp. vanilla
  1 loaf old bread, white, wheat or dark, cubed

Blend everything but the bread with a beater until smooth. Add the bread and toss.

Pour into buttered soufflé, casserole dish or loaf pan. Bake for 15-20 minutes or until done.

Serve warm with the Jack Daniels sauce over the bread pudding.

Jack Daniels Sauce

  1 stick sweet butter
  1 cup sugar
  ½ cup coffee
  ½ cup cream
  1 cup dark Karo syrup
  2 Tbsps. whiskey
  1 tsp. vanilla

Melt the butter and sugar in a large saucepan until caramelized. Add the coffee and bring to a boil. Reduce heat and add the cream, stirring constantly. Add the Karo syrup, whiskey and vanilla.

Serve at room temperature.

CARMEL VALLEY: RURAL ROOTS

WITHOUT THE PRECIOUS water of the Carmel River, the Monterey Peninsula could not have grown.

The Pacific Improvement Company, owned by the Big Four of railroad fame, needed a large supply of water for its Hotel Del Monte. The massive resort hotel contained hundreds of guest rooms and featured the Roman Plunge, an immense swimming pool.

About 700 Chinese laborers were hired to build the original San Clemente Dam and to lay twelve-inch pipe to bring the water out of the valley.

Because of the ready availability of water and its fertile soil, Carmel Valley became an agricultural and cattle center. Today, the cowboy character of the early valley remains, mingling with upscale homes, lush golf courses, posh resorts, tennis clubs, fruit orchards, and sprawling shopping complexes at its mouth.

LARGE TRACTS OF LAND were granted by Mexico after its freedom from Spain in 1822. After the end of the U.S.-Mexican War in 1848, the land grants had to be confirmed by a California board.

Four land grants involved Carmel Valley. Canada de la Segunda, 4,366 acres near the entrance to the valley, were granted in 1836 to Lazaro Soto; the grant was confirmed to Andrew Randall et al in 1858. El Potrero de San Carlos, 4,306 acres, was granted to Fructuoso (no first name given) in 1837; the grant was confirmed in 1855 to Joaquin Gutierez and patented in 1862. Los Laureles, 6,624 acres, was granted to J.M. Boronda in 1839; the grant was confirmed to Boronda in 1856. Los Tularcitos, 26,581 acres in upper Carmel Valley, extending up Chupines Creek toward Tassajara Hot Springs, was granted in 1834 to Rafael Gomez; the grant was confirmed to his heirs in 1855.

THE SHELTERED VALLEY boasts temperatures 10 to 20° higher than the foggier coastal regions. Verdant meadows and a profusion of spring wildflowers nestle between oak-dotted mountains.

The valley stretches for about 26 miles from Highway 1 to the Jamesburg area. A wonderful place for a leisurely drive, the eastern end of the valley leads to the large Salinas Valley, its inland highways and enormous fields.

The farther one travels east along Carmel Valley Road, the easygoing rural atmosphere becomes more apparent. As the golf courses are left behind, the roads get curvier and the scenery becomes more unspoiled. Deep into the valley, cowboys' dented pickup trucks and expensive European sedans are more likely to share the roads.

The mouth of Carmel Valley, adjacent to Highway 1, features artichoke fields and two large shopping complexes, the Barnyard and the Crossroads. Each specializes in chic boutiques, specialty shops, a scattered array of restaurants, art galleries and masses of decorative flowers.

CARMEL VALLEY DATEBOOK: Fiesta de los Amigos, April; Carmel Valley Ranchers' Day, September.

THE COVEY RESTAURANT

FRENCH CUISINE
Quail Lodge
8205 Valley Greens Drive
Carmel, CA 93923
624-1581
Dinner nightly 6PM–9PM
AVERAGE DINNER FOR TWO: $55

IN A PEACEFUL country setting, minutes from Carmel, the Covey Restaurant is nestled among lavish golf fairways, a lake and landscaped grounds. Continental cuisine with a California touch is served by the lake, offering panoramic picture-window views of the lighted fountain and bridge.

Chef Bob Williamson combines quality with simplicity in his progressive creations.

Quail Lodge is perhaps best known as one of the very few Mobil 5 Star establishments in the United States, the only one between San Francisco and Los Angeles.

The resort conveys casual elegance with a passion for quality.

QUAIL LODGE

Menu for Eight

Leek and Onion Soup with Fresh Horseradish Cream
Roulade of Sole and Salmon in a Paprika Sauce
Dilled Cucumbers
Chicken Stuffed with Dates, Ham and Walnuts
Cranberry Glaze
Wild Rice
Chocolate and Grand Marnier Mousse Torte

Leek and Onion Soup with Fresh Horseradish Cream

Serves 8
Preparation Time: 30 Minutes

2 small leeks
2 Tbsps. butter
2 medium onions, diced
2 sprigs thyme (or ½ tsp. dried thyme)
3 qts. chicken broth
  Salt and white pepper to taste
1 cup whipping cream
⅔ cup horseradish, scraped (or 2 Tbsps. prepared horseradish)

Cut off the bottom third of the leeks and cut them across in regular slices about ³⁄₁₆″. Wash well in cold water, separating the "rings" in the process and chop.

Place the butter, chopped leeks, chopped onion and thyme in a heavy saucepan and sauté over moderate heat without coloring, approximately 3-6 minutes. Add the chicken broth. Bring to a boil and simmer 20 minutes. Season to taste with salt and pepper.

Whip the cream and gently fold in the horseradish.

Serve the soup in bowls and pass the horseradish cream separately.

Halibut and Salmon Roulade

Serves 8
Preparation Time: 30 Minutes

12 oz. halibut filet
12 oz. salmon filet
½ tsp. dill, chopped
1 cup flour
3 Tbsps. clarified butter
Salt and white pepper to taste
Parchment paper

Thinly slice the halibut and arrange the slices to form a rectangle 10″ × 8″ on a well-buttered parchment paper. Cover it with plastic wrap. Roll it gently with a rolling pin to form an even layer. Remove the wrap and sprinkle halibut with chopped dill. Season lightly with salt and pepper.

Thinly slice the salmon and arrange the slices on top of the halibut. Cover with wrap and roll again, very gently.

Remove the wrap, using the parchment paper to assist, and roll the fish to form a long roll. Wrapped in parchment, trim off the excess paper. Cut the roll into eight even pieces. Dust the exposed fish with flour.

Using a thick-bottomed 12″ sauté pan, heat the clarified butter until it forms a light haze. Stand the rings of fish in the pan and cook over moderate heat for 4 minutes each side, turning once.

Remove from the pan and peel off the parchment paper. Serve the roulade on the paprika sauce, garnished with the dilled cucumber.

Paprika Sauce

Preparation Time: 15 Minutes

2 strips bacon, diced
2 shallots, chopped
1 small carrot, chopped
1 rib celery, chopped
1 bay leaf
1 sprig marjoram (or ¼ tsp. dried)
2 Tbsps. sweet paprika
2 large tomatoes, chopped
2 cups clam juice
2 Tbsps. flour
1 cup sour cream
½ Tbsp. lemon juice
    Salt and pepper to taste

Place the bacon in a two qt. saucepan and heat gently until the bacon starts to crisp, approximately 3-4 minutes.

Add the shallots, carrot, celery, bay leaf and marjoram. Cover the pan and sauté the vegetables on moderate heat for 3-4 minutes without coloring. Remove from the heat and mix in the paprika. Add the tomato and clam juice. Return to the heat and bring to a boil. Cover and simmer for 15 minutes.

Mix the flour and sour cream together and whisk into the simmering liquid. Season with salt and pepper to taste. Add the lemon juice and cook 5 minutes. Strain.

For a richer sauce incorporate 2-3 Tbsps. unsalted butter.

Dilled Cucumbers

Serves 8
Preparation Time: 15 Minutes

 1 medium English cucumber
 2 Tbsps. butter
 ½ tsp. sugar
 ¼ cup white wine
 1 tsp. chopped dill
    Salt and pepper to taste

Cut the cucumber lengthwise into four even pieces. Remove the seeds. Make a strip along the outside of each piece with a peeler. Cut the cucumbers crosswise into 4 sections with a small knife and shape each piece into a long oval.

Heat a 10″ skillet and add the butter and cucumber. Add the sugar and toss the cucumbers until they are shiny. Add the wine and dill. Cover and cook gently until the cucumbers soften slightly, 3-4 minutes. Remove the lid and evaporate the remaining liquid over high heat, constantly tossing the cucumbers. Season lightly with salt.

Use the dill cucumbers to garnish the roulade.

Chicken with Date and Walnut Stuffing

Serves 8
Preparation Time: One Hour (note stock cooking time)

Four 4 lb. large frying chickens or range hens
  2 ribs of celery
  1 leek
  1 medium onion
  2 bay leaves
  2 sprigs thyme (or ¼ tsp. dried thyme)
1-inch piece ginger root
1¼ gallon water

Remove the legs from the hens and reserve for another use. Cut the winglets off, just inside the second joint. Pull the skin off. Remove the wishbone and cut off the breasts, leaving the wing bone attached to the breast. Refrigerate breasts while you prepare the stock, sauce and stuffing.

Stock

Make a chicken stock with the carcass, winglets and trimmings by placing them in a stew pan with assorted seasonal vegetables, water and aromatics. Bring the mixture to a boil and simmer 2½ hours. Strain and skim. Reduce liquid to approximately 1 cup.

Date and Walnut Stuffing

1 cup pitted dates, coarsely chopped
⅔ cup walnuts
1 Tbsp. shallots, chopped
2 Tbsps. parsley, chopped
½ cup ham, chopped
⅔ cup white breadcrumbs
⅛ tsp. black pepper
3 Tbsps. clarified butter

Place all ingredients except the breadcrumbs in a food processor and blend together in short "pulses". Do not overprocess. Blend in the breadcrumbs.

Place the chicken breasts, skin side down, on the cutting board. Lift the "tenderloin" or filets from each breast. Flatten the breasts and filets with a meat mallet.

Put some of the stuffing on each breast. Cover it with the filets and fold over the breast meat to form a nice thin "package". Season with salt and pepper and dust with flour.

Heat 3 Tbsps. clarified butter in a heavy flat sauté pan. Place the breasts, folded side down, in the pan. This will seal the closure.

To serve, put wild rice in the center of each plate and surround it with cranberry glaze. Place a chicken breast on top of the rice.

Cranberry Glaze

4 cups cranberries
2 cups water
2 Tbsps. sugar (or more to taste)
1 cup chicken stock
1 Tbsp. arrowroot in 2 Tbsps. water
3 Tbsps. butter, unsalted
   Salt and pepper to taste

Boil the cranberries, water and sugar together until the fruit is soft. Strain. Reduce the liquid to approximately 1 cup.

Add the reserved chicken stock. Thicken with the arrowroot. Whisk in the unsalted butter.

Season to taste with salt and pepper.

Wild Rice

1 cup wild rice
2 cups water
   Salt to taste

After briefly rinsing rice under tap water, bring the ingredients to a boil. Cover and simmer for 40 minutes. Do not remove the lid. Turn off the heat, and allow to set, covered, a few more minutes. Fluff prior to serving.

Chocolate and Grand Marnier Mousse Torte

Serves 12
Preparation Time: 45 Minutes (note refrigeration time)

4 cups soft cake crumbs
2 tsps. orange zest
4 Tbsps. clarified butter
2 Tbsps. Grand Marnier

Mix the ingredients together and press evenly onto the bottom of a 12″ tart pan with a removable base. Set aside.

Mousse

12 oz. Swiss chocolate
⅓ cup water
⅔ cup sugar
3 Tbsps. soft butter (unsalted)
5 egg yolks
⅓ cup strong coffee
3 Tbsps. Grand Marnier
3 egg whites
1½ cups whipping cream

Slowly melt the chocolate over a double boiler, taking care that it does not get wet.

Boil the water and sugar together for 3 minutes. Add the butter, egg yolks, coffee and Grand Marnier and cook carefully until it thickens to a creamy consistency. Remove from the heat.

Add the melted chocolate and whisk in. Whip the egg whites and fold in. Whip the cream and fold in.

Pour the mousse into the tart pan and chill one hour.

Run a small hot knife around the edge of the tart pan to loosen from the mold. Smooth the edges of the mousse with a hot palette knife. Chill while you prepare the frosting.

Frosting

12 oz. Swiss chocolate
1½ cups cream
½ cup strong coffee
2 Tbsps. Grand Marnier
½ cup soft butter

Finely chop the chocolate. Set aside

Boil the cream and coffee together. Remove from the heat and add the chocolate. Work well with a wooden spoon until the chocolate is fully blended. Add the Grand Marnier.

Remove from the heat and whisk in the soft butter. Let the mixture cool before using a pastry bag to decorate the torte.

THE RIDGE RESTAURANT

FRENCH/CALIFORNIA CUISINE
Robles del Rio Lodge
200 Punta Del Monte
Carmel Valley, CA 93924
659-0170
Lunch daily 11:30AM–2PM
Dinner nightly 5:00 PM–9PM
AVERAGE DINNER FOR TWO: $40

THE RIDGE RESTAURANT at Robles del Rio Lodge in Carmel Valley offers spectacular romantic vistas from its mountaintop perch. The Ridge is a legendary favorite with visitors, locals and guests who cherish the opportunity to experience world-class cuisine in a European setting.

Five-star, Swiss born and trained chef/owner Andre Lengacher has combined French and California cuisines to please the palate. In addition to fine dining nightly, the Ridge also offers delicious lunchtime fare as well as an extensive wine list which includes outstanding California and French varietals.

Enjoy tempting entrees such as Hazelnut Crusted Salmon in a Tomato Ginger Coulis, Southwestern Chicken Breasts in a Red Pepper Tequila Sauce with Polenta and Prime Rib of Pork seasoned with Thai spices and Coconut Orzo.

Chef Andre is known for his gracious hospitality and, when time permits, he delights in coming out of his busy kitchen to meet and greet his guests.

Three Onion Soup with Gruyère Crust

Serves 6
Preparation Time: 45 Minutes

8 Tbsps. (1 stick) butter
2 Maui onions, sliced ⅜" thick
2 Bermuda onions, sliced ⅜" thick
3 Spanish onions, sliced ⅜" thick
2 oz. Wild Turkey whiskey
2 Tbsps. black pepper
2 Tbsps. thyme, dried
1 Tbsp. Worcestershire sauce
2 qts. beef stock
6 slices sourdough bread, ½" thick, toasted
6 slices Gruyère cheese, ¼" thick

In a medium stock-pot, melt the butter, then sauté the onions slightly in butter until they just start to cook. Stir in the Wild Turkey, black pepper and thyme. Cover and reduce the heat, allowing the onions to sweat for 15 minutes.

Uncover and add the beef stock and Worcestershire sauce. Increase the heat and return the soup to a boil.

Pour the soup into heavy soup bowl or crocks. Top the soup with the toasted bread and the Gruyère cheese. Heat under a broiler until the cheese is golden brown.

Scallops in Fresh Basil and Roma Tomatoes over Fettucine

Serves 6
Preparation Time: 30 Minutes

24 oz. large sea scallops, drained
 1 lb. spinach fettucine
 1 lb. egg fettucine
 3 Tbsps. olive oil
 3 garlic cloves, chopped
 2 Tbsps. fresh basil, chopped
 6 Roma tomatoes, diced
 ⅓ cup white cooking wine
 ¼ cup chicken stock
    Grated Parmesan cheese

Rinse and drain the scallops. Set aside.

Cook the fettucine in boiling, salted water, according to package directions. Drain, rinse and cover to keep hot.

In a medium sauté pan, heat the olive oil until very hot, but not smoking. Add the scallops carefully, allowing each side of the scallops to brown. When scallops are half-cooked, add the garlic, basil and tomatoes. Toss slightly, then deglaze the pan with white wine. Add the chicken stock and allow to simmer until the flavors are combined and the scallops are thoroughly cooked.

Divide into 6 portions and serve over the warm fettucine. Top with the grated Parmesan cheese.

Rack of Lamb

Serve 6
Preparation Time: 30 Minutes
Pre-heat oven to 350°

    3 lamb racks
    2 Tbsps. olive oil
      Small bunch fresh rosemary, chopped
  ½ cup whole grain white wine mustard
  ½ cup brandy
    1 shallot, finely chopped
    1 cup lamb demi-glace
  ¾ cup heavy cream
      Salt and pepper to taste

Sprinkle the lamb rack with salt and pepper. Sear the lamb in hot oil until the juices are just sealed, but not cooked through. Remove from heat.

In a mixing bowl, combine the rosemary with ¼ cup mustard. Coat the lamb rack with the mustard mixture and place in a shallow baking dish. Roast in a pre-heated 350° oven to desire doneness. Allow about 12 to 13 minutes per pound for medium-rare. Check the temperature with a probe thermometer.

While the lamb racks are roasting, in a small sauce pot reduce the brandy with the shallots by one third. Add the demi-glace, reserved ¼ cup mustard and heavy cream and reduce again by one third. Set aside.

When the lamb racks are done, cut the rack into 6 chop portions. Divide each rack into 2 portions.

Serve on a platter with the sauce under the chops.

BIG SUR:
SEACOAST SUPREME

THE STUNNING BEAUTY of Big Sur extends 75 miles from Point Lobos, just south to Carmel, to Santa Lucia, just north of the Hearst Castle at San Simeon.

That stretch along Highway 1 includes spectacular ocean vistas from the cliff-hugging road, redwoods creeping toward the coast, isolated beaches and coves where the roaring surf is one's only companion, lush state parks, a world-class spa, and exquisite homes tucked against the monumental cliffs.

Romantic couples who draw inspiration from being isolated amid stunning surroundings would be well advised to pause and relish the Big Sur coast.

POINT LOBOS, a state reserve just south of Carmel, is a great place to explore tide pools, watch whales from the cliffs, stroll paths that curl around twisted Monterey cypresses, spy on colonies of sea otters, and listen to the choirs of sea lions that congregate on the offshore rocks. Whaler's Cove, site of an old whaling station (a cabin on the shore has floor joists made out of whale ribs), is now a scuba-diving paradise. The languid inlet also boasts a history of shipwrecks, gold mining, smuggling, and was the site of an abalone cannery.

SCHOLARS SAY that Robert Louis Stevenson used the rugged coast of Point Lobos as the model for Treasure Island.

Palo Colorado Canyon contains a twisting, sun-speckled road that meanders around coastal redwood trees. An impressive side trip, the canyon takes the visitor to a quiet world of cool ferns and giant trees. Be

The Big Sur cliffs are a great spot for whale watching.

sure you take your time driving the road; it's narrow and curvy, but worth the leisurely trip.

Bixby Creek Bridge, originally known as the Rainbow Bridge, is one of the world's highest single span concrete bridges: it's over 260 feet high and over 700 feet long. The graceful bridge seldom fails to lure photographers.

It is said that actor Orson Welles bought the site of Nepenthe for sexy film siren Rita Hayworth. It is doubtful she ever took possession of the wonderful property, but it has flourished ever since.

The Esalen Spa got its start with an old Indian telling tales of a miraculous spring along the coast. Tom Slate, a young man crippled with arthritis, was transported over the difficult trail to the hot mineral baths. Slate was cured, so he bought the springs and surrounding acreage and Esalen was born.

The Big Sur Marathon, held in May, pits long-distance runners against the ups and downs of the Coast Highway. The finish line is at Rio Road, at the mouth of Carmel Valley.

BIG SUR DATEBOOK: Big Sur Marathon, May; Big Sur River Run, October.

SIERRA MAR

POST RANCH INN
CALIFORNIA CUISINE
Highway One
Big Sur
667-2200
Dinner nightly 6PM–10PM
Non-guests must make prior reservations
AVERAGE DINNER FOR TWO: $90
Room Rates $245–$450

LOOK AROUND YOU. From the dramatic coastline below where the Pacific Ocean crashes against the rocks, to the rugged wilderness that stretches into the distant mountains, all of this was once the Post Ranch homestead, settled in 1860 by William Brainard Post.

Each of the 30 guest units on the 98 acres is named after and tells the story of the spirited and courageous settlers. The buildings have been created to strike a fine balance with the forces of nature. Each unit offers the utmost in relaxation with bathtub/Jacuzzi, fireplace, stereo system and in-room massage tables.

The Post Ranch Inn restaurant, Sierra Mar, serves fresh regional California cuisine nightly. Continental breakfasts and picnic lunches are available to guests only. Perched on the edge of the Pacific Ocean, Sierra Mar offers extraordinary dining in a dramatic setting.

Post Ranch Inn
AT BIG SUR

Menu for Four

Potatoes Stuffed with Smoked Trout Mousse
Fettucine with Olive, Tomato and Basil
Venison with Currant and White Raisins

Small Red Potatoes Stuffed with Smoked Trout Mousse and Caviar

Serves 4
Preparation Time: 45 Minutes

- 12 egg-sized red potatoes
- 1 side smoked trout
- ½ cup cream cheese
- 1 Tbsps. prepared horseradish
- 1 tsp. dill, chopped
- Squeeze of lemon juice
- 2 Tbsps. American caviar
- Dill sprigs for garnish

Boil potatoes in salted water until soft. Plunge immediately into ice water. When cold, remove and pat dry. Cut in half and cut a small slice off the bottom of each piece so they set nicely on a plate. Scoop out a small amount of potato with melon baller. Sprinkle potatoes with salt and pepper and set aside.

In a food processor, soften cream cheese. Add trout, horseradish, dill, salt, pepper and lemon juice. Place mousse in a pastry bag fitted with fluted tip and pipe onto the potatoes. Garnish with a small amount of caviar and a dill sprig.

Fettucine Noodles with Olive, Tomato and Basil

Serves 4
Preparation Time: 30 Minutes

½ lb. Kalamata olives, pitted
1⅓ cup olive oil
1 Tbsp. garlic, chopped
1 tsp. fresh ground white pepper
1 lb. ripe tomatoes
2 big bunches basil
6 garlic cloves
Juice of 1 lemon
2 Tbsps. pinenuts, toasted
¼ cup Parmesan cheese, grated
1 lb. good quality fettucine noodles

Prepare the olive tapenade by puréeing the olives, ⅓ cup olive oil, 1 Tbsp. chopped garlic and white pepper in a blender or food processor. Set aside.

Prepare the tomato concasse by peeling the tomatoes, then seeding and chopping finely. Cook the tomatoes in a heavy-bottomed pan, stirring frequently, until all liquid has evaporated, leaving a thick tomato paste. Season with salt and pepper. Set aside.

Prepare the pesto by puréeing basil leaves with 6 garlic cloves, olive oil, lemon juice, salt and pepper. Purée well, add pinenuts and Parmesan cheese. Purée again and reserve.

Cook noodles in plenty of boiling salted water until al dente. Chill immediately in ice water. Drain well. Toss with a little olive oil to prevent noodles from sticking.

To assemble pasta, toss with olive tapenade, tomato concasse and pesto. Garnish with Parmesan cheese.

Roast Rack of Venison with Currant and White Raisins

Serves 4
Preparation Time: 1½ Hours (note marinating time)

1 rack of venison
1 bottle red wine
3 Tbsps. juniper berries, crushed
2 Tbsps. black pepper, cracked
1 onion, chopped
1 Tbsp. garlic, chopped
1 bunch parsley, chopped
2 bay leaves
2 cups port wine
2 cups venison marinade
1 qt. veal stock
1 Tbsp. peppercorns
10 mushrooms, chopped
¼ cup mixed currants and white raisins

Marinate the venison overnight in red wine, 2 Tbsps. juniper berries, black pepper, onion, garlic, parsley and 1 bay leaf.

Two hours before serving time, make the sauce using port wine with the venison marinade. Reduce this to 1 cup, then add the veal stock, peppercorns, 1 Tbsp. juniper berries, mushrooms, 1 bay leaf, currants and raisins. Strain through a fine strainer, reserve currants and raisins and set aside.

45 minutes before serving time, pre-heat oven to 350.° Remove venison rack from marinade and pat dry. Season with salt and pepper.

Film a large sauté pan with olive oil and heat to high. Sear the venison rack all over until browned. Place on a roasting rack in oven and cook until rare, about 20–25 minutes or thermometer registers 120.° Remove to a warm place and allow to rest for 15–20 minutes.

Slice into portions and nap with sauce, sprinkled with currants and raisins.

VENTANA

CALIFORNIA CUISINE
Big Sur, CA
93920
624-4812
Lunch daily 12noon–3PM
Dinner 6PM–9PM
AVERAGE DINNER FOR TWO: $60

DINE A THOUSAND feet above the Pacific in Ventana's elegantly appointed restaurant, where windows reveal a dramatic expanse of ocean and mountains.

The award-winning menu offers exceptional luncheons and dinners every day of the year, in an atmosphere of airy natural cedar and fireside warmth or on the beautifully landscaped terrace. The romance of view and food make it one of the world's great dining experiences.

The inn is a retreat for discriminating lovers. The high ceilings, fireplaces, ocean view balconies, saunas and Japanese hot baths make this country inn an unusually romantic and spectacularly beautiful place to be.

°Menu for Four

Seared Rabbit with Penne Pasta
Oak-Smoked Salmon with Lemon Crème Fraîche
Lobster and Mascarpone Ravioli
with Tomato Vinaigrette and Chanterelles

Seared Rabbit with Penne Pasta

Serves 4
Preparation Time: 45 Minutes

1 rabbit (2 to 3 lbs.)
   Salt and pepper to taste
¼ cup extra virgin olive oil
2 Tbsps. garlic, minced
1 Tbsp. rosemary
1 cup red wine
1 lb. penne pasta
2 cans premium peeled tomatoes

Rinse the rabbit well, pat dry and cut into twelve pieces. Reserve the liver and cut into small pieces. Season with salt and pepper. Heat a skillet or sauté pan with olive oil and brown the rabbit on all sides.

Remove the rabbit from skillet and sauté the garlic and liver with the rosemary. Deglaze with red wine. Add the tomatoes and rabbit and reduce sauce by half on low heat, approximately 20 minutes.

Bring a large pot of fresh water to a boil. Add the penne, and cook at a rolling boil until just tender.

Drain the pasta and toss it in the bowl with the sauce until well coated. Serve immediately.

Oak-Smoked Salmon
with Lemon Crème Fraîche

Serves 6
Preparation Time: 45 Minutes (note marinating time)

1 side fresh 12–14 lb. salmon,
   skin left on, halved lengthwise
1 box coarse (kosher) salt
1 cup creme fraiche
1 Tbsp. grated lemon zest
   Salt to taste
1 Tbsp. chives

Wipe the salmon dry with paper towels. Score the skin, making four shallow incisions with a knife. Cover the salmon skin with the salt and wrap the salmon with plastic wrap. Place the salmon in the refrigerator, placing a large platter or chopping board over the salmon, and weight it with a brick or heavy can. Allow the salmon to marinate for 24 hours.

While the salmon is marinating, prepare the lemon crème fraîche by whipping the crème fraîche in a mixing bowl until stiff peaks form. Add the lemon zest, salt and chives. Set aside and refrigerate until needed.

After the salmon has finished marinating, remove the weights and plastic wrap. Using a dry towel, remove all of the salt.

Smoke the salmon in a smoker for 45 minutes.

When you are ready to serve it, slice the salmon very thin on the bias. Serve with the lemon crème fraîche.

Lobster and Mascarpone Ravioli with Tomato Vinaigrette and Chanterelles

Serves 4
Preparation Time: One Hour

½ lb. mascarpone
1 tsp. grated lemon zest
1 Tbsp. basil, slivered
½ lb. lobster, cooked, diced
  Salt and white pepper to taste
  Won ton wrappers
¼ lb. sun-dried tomatoes
¼ cub whole basil leaves
¼ cup + 2 Tbsps. extra virgin olive oil
 2 Tbsps. balsamic vinegar
¼ cup vegetable stock
¼ cup chanterelles
 1 sprig rosemary

To prepare the raviolis, combine the mascarpone, lemon zest, basil and lobster. Salt and pepper to taste.

Place a teaspoon of the mixture onto each won ton skin. Seal the edges of each won ton with tepid water. Cover the filling with another won ton skin. Press firmly around edges to seal. Repeat with the remaining won tons. Set aside.

Prepare the vinaigrette by combining the tomatoes, whole basil, ¼ cup olive oil, balsamic vinegar and vegetable stock in a blender. Process at high speed until vinaigrette is emulsified. Season to taste with salt and pepper.

Slice the chanterelles and sauté in 2 Tbsps. olive oil. Add the rosemary sprig, salt and white pepper to taste. Remove from the heat.

Bring a large pot of salted water to a boil. Drop in the ravioli and cook until they rise to the surface, about 1 to 2 minutes. Drain.

Place the raviolis in a serving bowl and drizzle with the vinaigrette. Add the chanterelles around the raviolis. Serve immediately.

Monterey County Wines: A Pleasant Surprise

Franciscan friars planted the county's first wine grapes almost 200 years ago in the Spanish mission at Soledad.

But it took until 1960 for Monterey County to realize its full potential as a wine-producing region, when established wineries such as Chalone, Wente, Mirassou and Paul Masson expanded their plantings to the county. Now, Monterey contains 35,000 acres of grapes.

The county's vintners tend to favor varietals that consistently yield good to superior wines. Among the outstanding varieties with dozens of medals in state and national competitions are Cabernet Sauvignon, Chardonnay, Pinot Noir, Johannisberg Riesling, Pinot Blanc, Chenin Blanc, Gewurztraminer and Champagne.

Other regions of the state may still be better known for their wines, but fine wines with the Monterey appellation are reaping widespread praise. Monterey County wines display distinctive qualities, including unusual fruitiness, well-developed color and good sugar-acid balance.

The growing success of the county's wines is attributed to three key elements: near-perfect climate, fertile soil and a solid blend of traditional and scientific methods used by growers and winemakers.

In addition, some of the more select wineries tend to take greater care in producing smaller volumes of distinctive wines.

We encourage you to savor Monterey County wines. You may be very pleasantly surprised.

In photo above, a group of neighbors made homemade wine in Monterey in the '20s. But things have changed since then and fine wine grapes like those at right are making Monterey County an important wine area.

BARGETTO WINERY

700 Cannery Row Suite L
Monterey, CA 93940
373-4053
Open daily

THE BARGETTO WINERY was founded in 1933 by brothers
Philip and John Bargetto who had emigrated from the Piedmonte region
of northern Italy. Today, the winery is operated by the third generation of
Bargettos, who have the same lifelong ambition as their forefathers—to
produce wines of superior quality. Bargetto is not ony regarded as one of
California's premier producers of fine varietals, but also of the country's
finest natural fruit wines such as Raspberry, Olallieberry and Apricot.

LAWRENCE J. BARGETTO

CENTRAL COAST

Cypress · Chardonnay

Shrimp in Gewurztraminer Dijon Sauce

Serves 4
Preparation Time: 15 Minutes
(Adapted from Patricia Ballard's "Fine Wine and Food")

3 Tbsps. olive oil
3 Tbsps. butter
4 large cloves garlic, cut in half
1 cup Bargetto Gewurztraminer
2 Tbsps. Dijon mustard
2 lbs. shrimp, shelled and deveined

In a large, heavy skillet, heat oil and butter until haze forms. Add garlic and cook until browned. Remove garlic and discard. Add wine and bring to a boil. Lower heat and whisk in mustard. Add shrimp and cook until shrimp are pink (3 to 4 minutes). Serve with lots of sourdough bread for dunking in the sauce and, of course, drink the rest of the Gewurztraminer with the shrimp.

Raspberry Salad Dressing

Preparation Time: 10 Minutes

1 Tbsp. blue cheese
2 Tbsps. Raspberry Wine
2 Tbsps. Chef Luigi Wine Vinegar
2 Tbsps. almond pieces
½ cup olive oil

Blend the first four ingredients until smooth. Add the olive oil slowly until the mixture is emulsified.

CHALONE VINEYARD

P.O. Box 855
Soledad, CA 93960
Telephone Orders (415)546-7755
Winery tours by appointment

CHALONE VINEYARD IS remotely situated in the Gavilan Mountains to the east of the Salinas Valley. Here they produce small lots of 100% varietal Estate Bottled wines from grapes grown on the property.

The vines at Chalone Vineyard must cope with an extremely dry climate and a sparse limestone soil. The sheer difficulty of growing grapes here makes one pause. The obstacles include deer, rabbits, gophers, birds, and low rainfall. Each vine yields but two bottles of wine; thus the flavors are concentrated and the varietal character intensified.

All white wine fermentations are conducted entirely in barrels in underground cellars, designed after a typical French cave, requiring no air-conditioning to keep it cool.

As vintage succeeded vintage, Chalone learned that winemaking is a natural process that needs intelligent and sensitive guidance.

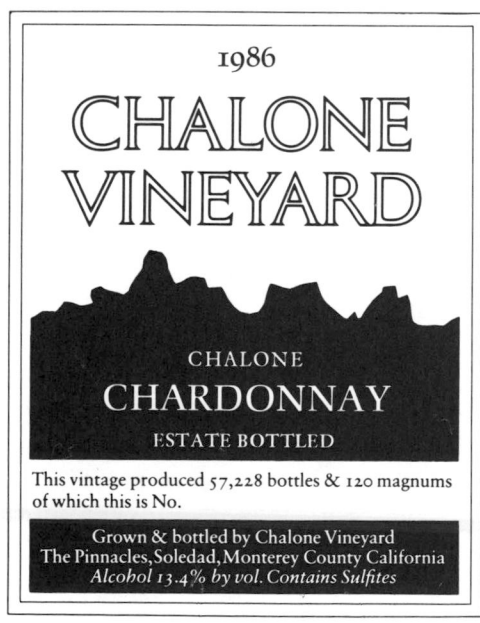

1986

CHALONE VINEYARD

CHALONE
CHARDONNAY
ESTATE BOTTLED

This vintage produced 57,228 bottles & 120 magnums of which this is No.

Grown & bottled by Chalone Vineyard
The Pinnacles, Soledad, Monterey County California
Alcohol 13.4% by vol. Contains Sulfites

Poached Salmon in Chardonnay

Serves 4 to 6
Preparation Time: 45 Minutes
Pre-heat oven to 400°

5-7 lbs. fresh whole salmon
1 Tbsp. sweet butter
6 sprigs of fresh dill weed
1 lemon, sliced
1 bottle Chalone Chardonnay

Clean salmon thoroughly and remove scales. Place in lightly buttered pan, arranging half of the sliced lemon and dill inside fish. Pour half the bottle of Chardonnay over fish and dot with remaining butter. Arrange several slices of lemon and dill on outside of salmon.

Cover and bake for approximately 30 minutes or until cooked to taste.

Enjoy the remainder of the Chardonnay while you wait for the fish to cook.

CHATEAU JULIEN

8940 Carmel Valley Road
Carmel Valley, CA 93922
624-2600
Tour and tasting room

CAREFULLY ORCHESTRATED CELLARING and bottle aging are instrumental parts of the Chateau Julien story. The philosophy of quality rather than quantity is stressed.

The Chateau is a delightful place to stop for a visit. Set against a backdrop of the steeply rugged Carmel Valley hills; the winery is elegantly French in style, with a distinctive California character.

Stuffed Trout with Asparagus

Serves 4
Preparation Time: 35 Minutes
Pre-heat oven to 350°

6 celery stalks, finely chopped
2 cups small mushrooms, finely chopped
½ cup blanched almonds, finely chopped
2 cups canned baby clams, chopped
  Pinch tarragon
  Pinch sweet basil
4 cloves garlic, finely chopped
8 strips medium cooked bacon, chopped
4 boned trout
8 Tbsps. butter
2 Tbsps. reserved bacon drippings
6 Tbsps. flour
1 cup clam juice
1 cup Sauvignon Blanc
1½ lbs. fresh asparagus

In a medium-sized bowl mix together chopped celery, mushrooms and almonds. Fold in clams, tarragon, basil, garlic and chopped bacon. Stuff trout with the mixture and seal fish with small skewers or toothpicks.

In an 8 × 14-inch glass baking dish place 4 Tbsps. butter. Put dish in preheated 350° oven until butter is melted. Remove pan from oven and gently place the stuffed trout in the baking dish. Cover dish with aluminum foil with one corner folded back slightly. Bake for 20 to 25 minutes.

While trout is baking, place 4 Tbsps. butter in medium-sized frying pan with the bacon drippings. Heat to slightly bubbling. Stir in flour and continue to stir while thickening. Lower heat. Slowly stir in clam juice and Sauvignon Blanc. Add more liquid if sauce is too thick.

Steam asparagus until tender. When trout is cooked, place it and the asparagus on a platter. Pour sauce over both.

DURNEY VINEYARD

P.O. Box 222016
Carmel, CA 93922
625-5433

DURNEY VINEYARD, a unique wine estate in Carmel Valley, is located about 20 miles inland from the Pacific Ocean. A micro climate, created by the mountains, which cradle the vineyards and winery, provides the ideal environment for the growth and production of award-winning vintage wines.

The vines, planted on gently rolling slopes, are naturally irrigated by underground springs. Traditional farming methods are utilized and no pesticides or herbicides are used in the cultivation of the vineyard.

The 82 acres of vineyards are part of the greater 1,200 acre property purchased and named by William and Dorothy Durney in 1954, Rancho Del Sueño, Ranch of Dreams.

Cabernet Lamb

Serves 4
Preparation Time: 40 Minutes (note marinating time)

1 **cup Durney Vineyard 1990 Cabernet Sauvignon**
½ **cup tamari sauce**
½ **cup fresh mint, chopped**
4 **large garlic cloves, crushed**
2 **Tbsps. fresh rosemary**
  Black pepper to taste
5 **lbs. leg of lamb, butterflied**

Combine the Cabernet with the tamari, mint, garlic, rosemary and pepper to make a marinade.

Place the lamb in a roasting pan and cover with the marinade. Refrigerate for 6 hours, turning the lamb often.

Prepare the barbecue to a medium low heat and grill the lamb, basting frequently, with the marinade. The lamb should be medium rare to rare after 20 minutes.

JEKEL VINEYARD

40155 Walnut Ave.
Greenfield, CA 93927
674-5522
Tour and tasting room

JEKEL VINEYARD IS a family-owned vineyard and winery. The vineyard was planted in 1972 on 140 acres of rocky loam, just west of Greenfield.

The winery produced its first wines in 1978. Their wines have been recognized for their consistent quality by the many awards they win each year.

Seafood Sausages

Preparation Time: 45 Minutes (note elapsed time)
Makes 20 sausages

½ lb. fresh small bay scallops
½ lb. ling cod, or other rock fish, fresh or smoked
½ lb. shrimp, peeled
½ lb. crab meat
½ lb. salmon, fresh or smoked
 6 eggs
 6 carrots diced
 8 shallots minced
 1 stalk celery chopped fine
 1 pepper, red or green, chopped
 6 oyster or shiitake mushrooms minced
 6 oz. Jekel Chardonnay
20 natural sausage casings

Grind the seafood in a food processor. Sauté the shallots, carrots, celery and pepper until soft. Blend the cooked vegetables and seafood mixture with the eggs, wine and mushrooms.

Stuff the mixture into the natural sausage casing. Sausages should set for 4 or more hours before poaching.

Sauce

1 quart fish or clam stock
8 oz. Jekel Chardonnay
1 pint cream

Combine fish stock and wine to poach the sausages for 10 minutes over medium heat. Remove sausages and add cream.

Pour sauce over sausages and serve.

JOULLIAN

20300 Cachagua Road
Carmel Valley, CA 93924
659-2035

CARMEL VALLEY, ONE of America's smallest and most unique winegrowing appellations, was selected by Joullian Vineyards because it produces some of the richest and most flavorful wines in California.

By planting numerous multi-clonal varietal blocks, each in a slightly different set of growing circumstances, Joullian Vineyards has endeavored to create extra-dimensional wines in the field as well as in the winery.

All Joullian wines receive extended bottle aging, usually a minimum of two years. The extra maturation period ensures that upon release, the wines have begun to develop their special Carmel Valley character, as well as extra smoothness, complexity and bouquet.

CARMEL VALLEY

Joullian Tri-Tips of Beef

Serves 4
Preparation Time: 45 Minutes (note marinating time)

⅔ cup soy sauce
¼ cup Joullian Cabernet Sauvignon
3 cloves garlic, minced
½ tsp. black pepper
2 Tbsps. fresh cilantro, chopped
2 whole tri-tips of beef

In a mixing bowl, combine the soy sauce, Cabernet, garlic, pepper and cilantro for the marinade.

Marinate the tri-tips for 1 hour before grilling or barbecuing to desired doneness.

LA REINA WINERY

P.O. Box 1344
Carmel, CA 93921
373-3294

THE BOUTIQUE-STYLE La Reina Winery was founded by Charles and Sandra Chrietzberg in 1984 in the small town of Gonzales in southern Monterey County.

Limiting production to Chardonnay only, the small winery quickly developed a following for its hand-crafted "Queen of Chardonnays."

While the winery cannot accommodate quests, you will find this enticing wine in area restaurants and retail stores.

La Reina

1986

MONTEREY COUNTY

CHARDONNAY

PRODUCED AND BOTTLED BY LA REINA, SAN MARTIN, CA
ALCOHOL 12.8% BY VOLUME   CONTAINS SULFITES

Chardonnay Mousse

Serves 6
Preparation Time: 15 Minutes (note refrigeration time)

>   1 cup La Reina Chardonnay
>   Juice of 2 lemons
>   Juice of 2 oranges
>   ¾ cup sugar
>   6 eggs
> 1½ tsps. gelatin powder
>   1 pt. whipping cream
>   Red grapes for garnish

Place the wine and sugar in a saucepan with the lemon and orange juice and bring to a boil.

Separate the eggs, placing the yolks in a stainless steel bowl. When the wine mixture boils, pour it over the egg yolks, stirring slightly. Add the gelatin and stir. Strain the mixture to cool.

Whip the cream and fold into the cooled mixture. Pour into wine glasses and set in the refrigerator for 1 hour.

Separate grapes into clusters of 3, dipping them into egg whites and then sugar. Place on top of the mousse for garnish.

MONTEREY PENINSULA WINERY

786 Wave Street
Monterey, CA 93940
372-4949
Tasting Room

MONTEREY PENINSULA WINERY produces hand-tended wines of character. As winemakers, they believe that wine is grown in the vineyard and that they are the stewards of nature while the wine is in their cellar.

The 1985 Chardonnay represents the second consecutive vintage from Sleepy Hollow. It is one of the northernmost vineyards in the Monterey appellation and less than 15 miles from Monterey Bay. The cooling ocean breezes insure a long, cool growing season which results in good acid structure at full ripeness.

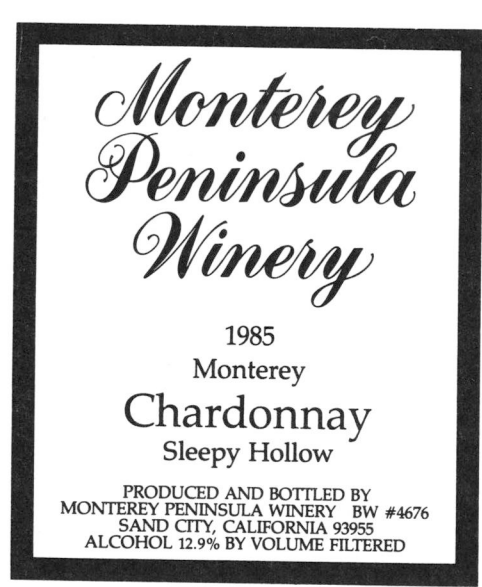

Monterey Peninsula Winery

1985
Monterey
Chardonnay
Sleepy Hollow

PRODUCED AND BOTTLED BY
MONTEREY PENINSULA WINERY   BW #4676
SAND CITY, CALIFORNIA 93955
ALCOHOL 12.9% BY VOLUME FILTERED

Marinated Shrimp

Serves 6
Preparation Time: 15 Minutes

36 medium to large shrimp
Crab boil (pre-packaged at supermarket)

Marinade

1 large egg yolk
¾ cup olive oil
¾ cup peanut oil
¾ cup red wine vinegar
1 Tbsp. shallots, chopped
3 Tbsps. parsley, chopped
3 Tbsps. chives, chopped

Devein and peel the shrimp. Boil with 3 Tbsps. crab boil in the water. Remove from the heat when they turn pink. Cool in water.

Whisk the egg yolk, oils, vinegar, and mustard. Add the shallots, parsley and chives.

Drain the shrimp and put them in a serving bowl. Pour marinade over the shrimp and refrigerate for at least 2 hours, turning several times.

Enjoy with a bottle of Monterey Peninsula Chardonnay.

THE MONTEREY VINEYARD

800 South Alta Street
Gonzales, CA 93926
675-2316
Open daily for tours and tastings

THE MONTEREY VINEYARD is located outside the town of Gonzales, 25 miles inland from Monterey Bay.

The Spanish-Mexican architecture emphasizes the heritage of northern California, and the stained glass windows in the winery illustrate the different grape varieties.

The grounds encompass a museum-quality gallery featuring a permanent exhibition of Ansel Adams' "Story of a Winery", a Visitor Center where all wines are available to taste, as well as a beautiful picnic area.

THE
MONTEREY
VINEYARD.®

Frittata with Spring Garden Vegetables

Serves 12
Preparation Time: 1½ Hours
Pre-heat oven to 350°

2 Tbsps. butter
¼ cup olive oil
1 yellow onion, diced
2 garlic cloves, crushed
1 carrot, sliced in rounds
2 parsnips, sliced into rounds
6 zucchini, sliced into rounds
3 crookneck squash, sliced into rounds
4-5 eggs
2 Tbsps. cream
¼ cup milk
1 Tbsp. basil
1 Tbsp. thyme
½ pound Monterey Jack cheese, grated
3 Tbsps. Parmesan cheese
Roasted red peppers
Green chiles, diced

In a non-stick pan, sauté the onions in butter and olive oil until they are transparent. Remove from the pan. Sauté garlic and vegetable rounds until tender.

In a bowl, combine eggs, cream, milk, spices, and cheeses.

Remove the vegetables from the heat and return the onions to the pan. Stir the egg mixture into the vegetables, blending quickly and thoroughly. Return the pan to the stove and heat (without sticking) until the frittata begins to set up, approximately 10 minutes. Transfer the pan to a pre-heated 350° oven for 1 hour, or until completely set and golden brown.

Remove the frittata from the oven; let cool before flipping it out onto a large serving platter. Garnish with diced roasted red peppers, diced green chiles, and extra Parmesan cheese.

To serve, cut into pie-shapped wedges.

PAUL MASSON VINEYARDS

P.O. Box 1852
Saratoga, CA 95070-0199
For Special Events and information
741-5183

PAUL MASSON VINEYARDS, California's oldest continuous wine producing company and America's sixth largest, dates back to 1852.

In 1905, Paul Masson built a great stone winery at his mountain vineyard, with foundations deep into the hillside to maintain constant cool temperatures for aging wine. The 1906 earthquake shook loose thousands of bottles of Masson Champagne from their racks but did not destroy the winery.

In 1958, a series of summer concerts, Music at the Vineyards, was inaugurated at an outdoor amphitheater for which the imposing winery serves as a backdrop; the much-expanded series now attracts 60,000 music-lovers annually.

MONTEREY COUNTY
CHARDONNAY
Vintage 1985

This aristocrat of white wines is pleasantly crisp with a fragrant bouquet and rich complex flavors. Serve chilled. Alc. 12% by Vol.

PAUL MASSON®

Cellared & Bottled by Paul Masson Vineyards, Gonzales, CA

Veal Rolls

Serves 6
Preparation Time: 1½ Hours

12 Veal slices, pounded paper thin (3 × 5 inches) and dusted
   with flour
12 slices Virginia ham
12 lettuce leaves
12 leaves fresh sage (or ¼ tsp. dried)
 3 Tbsps. breadcrumbs
 3 Tbsps. chopped black olives
 3 Tbsps. olive oil
   Salt and pepper to taste
4-5 Tbsps. unsalted butter
   Juice of 1 lemon
 1 cup Paul Masson Monterey County Chardonnay

Top each veal slice with Virginia ham, lettuce leaf and sage. Set
aside. Mix breadcrumbs and black olives with olive oil, salt and pepper.
Transfer some of the mixture to each veal slice. Roll up the meat tightly
(egg roll style) and fasten with a cooking string. Refrigerate covered for
15 minutes.

Over low heat, melt the butter in a skillet, add the veal rolls and
brown lightly for 3 minutes on each side. Add the lemon juice and
Chardonnay and continue cooking for 5 minutes more, covered over
medium heat.

Let cool in the pan. Remove the strings and refrigerate for 1 hour
before serving.

SMITH & HOOK WINERY

37700 Foothill Road
Soledad, CA 93960
678-2132
Tour and Tasting Room

SMITH & HOOK perches on the eastern slope of the Santa Lucia Mountains, overlooking the Salinas Valley. The vineyard was purchased in 1973 after an eleven-year search that spanned three continents in pursuit of the right combination of soil, climate and vineyard exposure. The estate was created out of two ranches totalling 652 acres.

Efforts were made to retain the ranch's rustic feeling. The old stable now serves as the winery. The lab is in the former tack room, and offices are in the bunkhouse where ranch-hands once bedded down.

Smith & Hook produces only one wine, an estate-bottled Cabernet Sauvignon. With seven grape-producing slopes on the Smith & Hook wine estate, the winemaker is able to craft a Cabernet Sauvignon with a structure that demonstrates unusual complexity and quality.

Cabernet Black Olive Pâté

Serves 6
Preparation Time: 30 minutes

 2 Tbsps. olive oil
 1 bunch scallions
 3 garlic cloves, crushed
 2 medium sized tomatoes
 1 cup black olives, minced
 ½ tsp. dill weed
1½ cups Smith & Hook Cabernet

Sauté scallions and garlic in oil until soft. Add the tomatoes, olives and dill weed. Cook on low heat, covered for 10 minutes. Pour in the Cabernet, bringing the mixture to a boil. Reduce heat and simmer for 20 minutes uncovered, until mixture reduces to the consistency of a soft pâté.

Cook and serve with crackers and assorted breads.

ROBERT TALBOTT VINEYARDS

P.O. Box 776
Gonzales, CA 93926
675-3000

TALBOTT VINEYARDS has consistently been acclaimed by consumer and critics alike as one of the top wine producers in the world. Talbott Chardonnay, at $25 a bottle retail, is 100 percent allocated every year before release.

Located five miles from Gonzales in the Santa Lucia Highlands, this newly relocated winery was carefully planned to fit into the farm scene. It was placed 16 feet down into the existing landscape and the exterior has a board and batten look. The building has a peaked roof with dormers and cupolas, which make it look like a big barn. The cupolas contain exhaust fans for warm air that can be opened at night for the fog to cool the building.

Talbott Vineyard & Winery is now going to the production of Pinot Noir. The first production will be small—just 400 cases for the first release in '93 and probably will be as well received as its Chardonnays.

TALBOTT

1990
Chardonnay
Monterey

PRODUCED & BOTTLED BY ROBERT TALBOTT VINEYARDS
GONZALES, CA. USA · WHITE TABLE WINE

Lobster Thermidor

Serves 6
Preparation Time: 30 Minutes
Pre-heat oven to 400°

¾ **cup butter**
½ **cup sifted all-purpose flour**
3 **cups warm cream**
2 **Tbsps. Talbott Chardonnay**
   Pinch of cayenne pepper
¼ **tsp. dry mustard**
½ **lb. fresh mushrooms**
3 **cups cooked lobster meat cut into 1-inch pieces**
1½ **tsps. salt**
¼ **cup grated Parmesan cheese, plus topping cheese**
   Vegetable flowers and parsley for garnish

Melt ½ cup butter, add flour to make paste, and then add cream, a little at a time, stirring constantly, and cook until thick. Sauté mushrooms in butter. Add the wine, pepper, mustard, mushrooms, lobster meat and ¼ cup cheese, and sauté for 5 minutes. If mixture is too thick, add more cream.

Pour into medium-sized casserole. Sprinkle top thickly with additional cheese and drizzle melted butter over cheese. Bake 15 minutes at 400°, then broil for several minutes until top is brown. Garnish center of casserole with vegetable flowers and parsley.

Serve with an herb rice, vegetable medley of broccoli, carrots and cauliflower, mixed salad with honey mustard dressing and a bottle of Talbott Chardonnay.

VENTANA VINEYARDS

2999 Monterey-Salinas Highway
Monterey, CA 93940
372-7415
Tasting Room

THE VINEYARD WAS planted in the early 1970's by Doug Meador whose innovative farming methods have brought him everything from wild acclaim to disbelieving looks. However controversial they may be, they are almost always successful.

This is evident not only in the many fine wines of Ventana but also in the number of great wines from other labels bearing the vineyard designation of Ventana Vineyards.

The winery was established in 1978 with great enthusiasm for a new region, a strong belief in the land, a vision of world class wines on the horizon. It was a well founded belief, as Ventana Vineyards Winery has produced many award winning wines that are just that... world class.

MONTEREY
SAUVIGNON BLANC
VENTANA VINEYARDS

PRODUCED AND BOTTLED BY VENTANA VINEYARDS
SOLEDAD, CALIFORNIA B.W. 4847 · ALCOHOL 13.4% BY VOLUME
PRODUCE OF U.S.A. · CONTAINS SULFITES

Figs in Sauvignon Blanc with Vanilla Ice Cream

Serves 4
Preparation time: 10 minutes (note elapsed time)

  8 ripe figs
1½ cups Ventana Sauvignon Blanc
  1 pt. whipping cream
  1 tsp. vanilla
    Vanilla ice cream
½ cup almonds

Place peeled figs cut in half in a flat bowl with Sauvignon Blanc and marinade overnight (at least 4 hours). Reserve the figs and marinade.

Whip the cream with vanilla and refrigerate.

To serve, arrange figs on a plate and top with vanilla ice cream. Pour the marinade over the figs adding the whipped cream. Sprinkle with chopped almonds and serve.

How You Can Measure Up...

LIQUID MEASURES

1 dash	6 drops
1 teaspoon (tsp.)	⅓ tablespoon
1 tablespoon (Tbsp.)	3 teaspoons
1 tablespoon	½ fluid ounce
1 fluid ounce	2 tablespoons
1 cup	½ pint
1 cup	16 tablespoons
1 cup	8 fluid ounces
1 pint	2 cups
1 pint	16 fluid ounces

DRY MEASURES

1 dash	less than ⅛ teaspoon
1 teaspoon	⅓ tablespoon
1 tablespoon	3 teaspoons
¼ cup	4 tablespoons
⅓ cup	5 tablespoons plus 1 teaspoon
½ cup	8 tablespoons
⅔ cup	10 tablespoons plus 2 teaspoons
¾ cup	12 tablespoons
1 cup	16 tablespoons

VEGETABLES AND FRUITS

Apple (1 medium)	1 cup chopped
Avocado (1 medium)	1 cup mashed
Broccoli (1 stalk)	2 cups florets
Cabbage (1 large)	10 cups, chopped
Carrot (1 medium)	½ cup, diced
Celery (3 stalks)	1 cup, diced
Eggplant (1 medium)	4 cups, cubed
Lemon (1 medium)	2 tablespoons juice
Onion (1 medium)	1 cup, diced
Orange (1 medium)	½ cup juice
Parsley (1 bunch)	3 cups, chopped
Spinach (fresh), 12 cups, loosely packed	1 cup cooked
Tomato (1 medium)	¾ cup, diced
Zucchini (1 medium)	2 cups, diced

MAIL ORDER SOURCES

If you are unable to locate some of the specialty food products used in *Monterey's Cooking Secrets*, you can order them from the mail order sources listed below. These items are delivered by UPS, fully insured and at reasonable shipping costs.

CHEESE

Sonoma Cheese Factory
2 Spain Street
Sonoma, CA 95476
800-535-2855
707-996-1931
Imported cheeses as well as Sonoma Jack, Onion Jack, Garlic Jack and Sonoma lite.

Ideal Cheese
1205 Second Ave.
New York, NY 10021
(212) 688-7579
Imported Italian cheeses.

Mozzarella Company
2944 Elm St.
Dallas, TX 75226
(800) 798-2654
(214) 741-4072
(214) 741-4076 fax
Goat cheese, mascarpone, mozzarella, pecorino, ricotta and other cheeses.

Tillamook County Creamery Association
P.O. Box 313
Tillamook, OR 97141
(503) 842-4481
(800) 542-7290
Over 30 types of cheeses, black wax cheese, and a hot jalapeo cheese.

CHOCOLATES AND CANDY

The Brigittine Monks Gourmet Confections
23300 Walker Lane
Amity, OR 97101
(503) 835-8080
(503) 835-9662 fax
Popular items are chocolate with nuts and pecan pralines.

Festive Foods
9420 Arroyo Lane
Colorado Springs, CO 80908
(719) 495-2339
Spices and herbs, teas, oils, vinegars, chocolate and baking ingredients.

COFFEE AND TEA

Brown & Jenkins Trading Co.
P.O. Box 2306
South Burlington, VT 05407-2306
(802) 862-2395
(800) 456-JAVA
Water-decaffeinated coffees, featuring over 30 blends such as Brown & Jenkins Special blend, Vermont Breakfast blend and Hawaiian Kona, in addition to 15 different flavors of teas.

Stash Tea Co.
P.O. Box 90
Portland, OR 97207
(503) 684-7944
(800) 826-4218
Earl Grey, herbal teas like peppermint, ruby mint, orange spice and licorice flavors.

DRIED BEANS AND PEAS

Corti Brothers
5801 Folsom Blvd.
Sacramento, CA 95819
(916) 736-3800
Special gourmet items such as imported extra-virgin olive oils, wines, exotic beans, egg pasta.

Dean & Deluca
560 Broadway
New York, NY 10012
(800) 221-7714
(212) 431-1691
Dried beans, salted capers, polenta, Arborio rice, dried mushrooms, dried tomatoes, Parmesan and reggiano cheeses, kitchen and baking equipment.

DRIED MUSHROOMS

Gold Mine Natural Food Co.
1947 30th St.
San Diego, CA 92102-1105
(800) 475-3663
Organic foods, dried foods, whole grain rice, Asian dried mushrooms, condiments and sweeteners.

FISH, CAVIAR AND SEAFOOD

Nelson Crab
Box 520
Tokeland, WA 98590
(206) 267-2911
(800) 262-0069
Fresh seafood as well as canned specialties such as salmon, shrimp and tuna.

Legal Sea Foods
33 Everett Street
Boston, MA 02134
(617) 254-7000
(800) 343-5804
Live lobsters, fresh filets and seafood steaks, clam chowder, little neck steamer clams, shrimp, smoked Scottish salmon and Beluga caviar.

FLOURS AND GRAINS

G.B. Ratto & Co. International Grocers
821 Washington Street
Oakland, CA 94607
(510) 832-6503
(800) 325-3483
Flours, rice, bulgar wheat, couscous, oils, and sun-dried tomatoes.

King Arthur Flour Baker's Catalogue
P.O. Box 876
Norwich, VT 05055
(800) 827-6836
Semolina flour, all types of flours, wheat berries, kitchen and baking equipment.

The Vermont Country Store
P.O. Box 3000
Manchester Center, VT 05255-3000
(802) 362-2400 credit card orders
(802) 362-4647 customer service
Orders are taken 24 hours a day.
Many different varieties of flour: whole wheat, sweet-cracked, stone-ground rye, buckwheat, cornmeal and many more. They also sell a variety of items which are made in Vermont.

FRUITS & VEGETABLES

Giant Artichoke
11241 Merritt St.
Castroville, CA 95012
(408) 633-2778
Fresh baby artichokes.

Lee Anderson's Covalda Date Company
51-392 Harrison Street (Old Highway 86)
P.O. Box 908
Coachella, CA 92236-0908
(619) 398-3441
Organic dates, raw date sugar and other date products. Also dried fruits, nuts and seeds.

Timber Crest Farms
4791 Dry Creek Road
Healdsburg, CA 95448
(707) 433-8251
Domestic dried tomatoes and other unsulfured dried fruits and nuts.

MEATS AND POULTRY

New Braunfels Smokehouse
P.O. Box 311159
New Braunfels, TX 78131-1159
(512) 625-7316
(800) 537-6932
A family-owned business since 1943, selling quality hickory smoked meats, poultry, and fish. They also sell lean summer sausages, bacon, and beef jerky.

Omaha Steaks International
P.O. Box 3300
Omaha, NE 68103
(800) 228-9055
Corn-fed Midwestern beef, filet mignon and boneless strips of sirloin.

Gerhard's Napa Valley Sausages
901 Enterprise Way
Napa, CA 94558
(707) 252-4116
Specializing in more than 26 types of fresh and smoked sausages: chicken apple, East Indian, turkey/chicken, Syrian lamb, kielbasa, Italian, Bavarian beerwurst, Cajun, duck with roasted almonds—and much more. They do not use cereal fillers, MSG or artificial flavors.

Deer Valley Farm
R.D. #1
Guilford, NY 13780
(607) 764-8556
Organically raised chicken, beef and veal. These meats are very low in fat and high in flavor.

PASTA

Morisi's Pasta
John Morisi & Sons, Inc.
647 Fifth Avenue
Brooklyn, NY 11215
(718) 499-0146
(800) 253-6044
Over 250 varieties available from this 50-year-old, family-owned gourmet pasta business.

PASTRY AND BAKED GOODS

Cafe Beaujolais Bakery
P.O. Box 730
Mendocino, CA 95460
(707) 937-0443
Panfortes, almond and hazelnut pastries as well as fruit cakes, jam, chocolate and home-made cashew granola.

SAFFRON

Vanilla Saffron Imports, Inc.
949 Valencia Street
San Francisco, CA 94110
(415) 648-8990
(415) 648-2240 fax
Saffron, vanilla beans and pure vanilla extract, dried mushrooms as well as herbs.

SPECIALTY FOODS AND FOOD GIFTS

China Moon Catalogue
639 Post St.
San Francisco, CA 94109
(415) 771-MOON (6666)
(415) 775-1409 fax
Chinese oils, peppers, teas, salts, beans, candied ginger, kitchen supplies, cookbooks.

Kozlowski Farms
5566 Gravenstein Highway
Forestville, CA 95436
(707) 887-1587
(800) 473-2767
Jams, jellies, barbecue and steak sauces, conserves, honeys, salsas, chutneys and mustards. Some products are non-sugared, others are in the organic line. You can customize your order from 65 different products.

SPICES AND HERBS

Penzey Spice House Limited
P.O. Box 1633
Milwaukee, WI 53201
(414) 768-8799
Fresh ground spices (saffron, cinnamon and peppers), bulk spices, seeds, and seasoning mixes.

Meadowbrook Herb Gardens
Route 138
Wyoming, RI 02898
(401) 539-7603
Organically grown herb seasonings, high quality spice and teas.

Rafal Spice Company
2521 Russell Street
Detroit, MI 48207
(800) 228-4276
(313) 259-6373
Seasoning mixtures, herbs, spices, oil, coffee beans and teas.

VINEGARS AND OILS

Williams-Sonoma
Mail Order Dept.
P.O. Box 7456
San Francisco, CA 94120-7456
(800) 541-2233 credit card orders
(800) 541-1262 customer service
Vinegars, oils, foods and kitchenware.

Community Kitchens
P.O. Box 2311, Dept. J-D
Baton Rouge, LA 70821-2311
(800) 535-9901
Vinegars and oil, in addition to meats, crawfish, coffees and teas.

Festive Foods
9420 Arroyo Lane
Colorado Springs, CO 80908
(719) 495-2339
Spices and herbs, teas, oils, vinegars, chocolate and baking ingredients.

Select Orgins
Box N
Southhampton, NY 11968
(516) 288-1382
(800) 822-2092
Oils, vinegars and rice.

RECIPE INDEX

ABOUT THE AUTHOR

KATHLEEN DEVANNA FISH, author of the popular "Secrets" series, is a gourmet cook and gardener who is always on the lookout for recipes with style and character.

In addition to *Cooking Secrets for Healthy Living*, the California native has written the award-winning *Great Vegetarian Cookbook*, *The Gardener's Cookbook*, *The Great California Cookbook*, *California Wine Country Cooking Secrets*, *San Francisco's Cooking Secrets*, *Monterey's Cooking Secrets*, *New England's Cooking Secrets*, *Cape Cod's Cooking Secrets*, *Pacific Northwest Cooking Secrets* and *Cooking and Traveling Inn Style*.

Before embarking on a writing and publishing career, she owned and operated three businesses in the travel and hospitality industry.

ROBERT FISH, award-winning photojournalist, produces the images that bring together the concept of the "Secrets" series.

In addition to taking the cover photographs, Robert explores the food and wine of each region, helping to develop the overview upon which each book is based.

Bon Vivant Press
A division of The Millennium Publishing Group
P.O. Box 1994
Monterey, CA 93942
800-524-6826
408-373-0592
408-373-3567 FAX

Send _____ copies of *Cooking Secrets for Healthy Living* at $15.95 each.

Send _____ copies of *Pacific Northwest Cooking Secrets* at $15.95 each.

Send _____ copies of *The Great California Cookbook* at $14.95 each.

Send _____ copies of *The Gardener's Cookbook* at $15.95 each.

Send _____ copies of *The Great Vegetarian Cookbook* at $15.95 each.

Send _____ copies of *California Wine Country Cooking Secrets* at $14.95 each.

Send _____ copies of *San Francisco's Cooking Secrets* at $13.95 each.

Send _____ copies of *Monterey's Cooking Secrets* at $13.95 each.

Send _____ copies of *New England's Cooking Secrets* at $14.95 each.

Send _____ copies of *Cape Cod's Cooking Secrets* at $14.95 each.

Add $3.00 postage and handling for the first book ordered and $1.50 for each additional book. Please add $1.08 sales tax per book, for those books shipped to California addresses.

Please charge my ☐ Visa ☐ MasterCard # _____

Expiration date _____ Signature _____

Enclosed is my check for _____

Name _____

Address _____

City _____ State _____ Zip _____

☐ This is a gift. Send directly to:

Name _____

Address _____

City _____ State _____ Zip _____

☐ Autographed by the author
   Autographed to _____